75th Technical Forum

75th Porcelain Enamel Institute Technical Forum

A Collection of Papers Presented at the 75th Porcelain Enamel Institute Technical Forum

May 14-16, 2013
Nashville, TN

Conference Director
Ben Stephen

Assistant Conference Director
David Latimer

Editors
Charles Baldwin
Renee Pershinsky

Publisher
Cullen Hackler

75th Porcelain Enamel Institute Technical Forum

Copyright 2014

Contents

Preface..ix

2013 PEI Officers..xi

2013 Technical Forum Committee..............................xiii

Past PEI Technical Forum Committee
Chairs..xv

2013 PEI Technical Forum Proceedings

Proceedings

Fracture Analysis of Laminate Porcelain Enamel Coatings......1
    Brad Potter, Kyla McKinley, Charles Baldwin

Characterization of Electrostatic Enamel Powders:
Study of Flow Properties Using Innovative
Measurement Methodology...21
    Pascal Delbaere, Johan De Soete

Improving the Substrate Wettability of an Enamel Through
the Use of a Surfactant..27
    Joe Melaro and Laura Hughes

Combining the Best Technologies for Powder Porcelain Enamel
Coating Applications...33
    John Carlson

Powder Porcelain Rooms, Blow-Off and Hanger Cleaners......39
    Mike Horton

Lean Six Sigma Overview...45
    Walt Skovron

Innovative Metallic Effect Frit for Oven Cavity - Pyrolytic KIRA..51
    Hidekazu Onishi, Hiroshi Iwamura, Shinichi Kuwae, Michael E. Tracey

Migration Testing of Enamels for Direct Contact with Drinking Water..55
    Eckhard Voss

Development of Durable Composites Incorporating Vitreous Enameled Metal..75
    Charles A. Weiss, Jr., Paul G. Allison, Robert D. Moser, Brett A. Williams, Stacy S. Holton and Philip G. Malone

Challenges and Outlook for Key Raw Materials................89
    Mark Doak, Patrick Palattella, Charles Baldwin

Twenty-First Century Cleaning Systems.......................111
    Ken Kaluzny

Cleaning and Metal Preparation for Porcelain Enameling.....115
    John O'Connor

Washer Fundamentals for Porcelain Enamel....................119
    Jeff Studnicka

Importance of Cleaning and Rinsing Prior to Enameling..123
    Suresh Patel

Rack Rotation for Process-to-Furnace Conveyor Transfer....135
    Richard A. Dooley

Understand and Interpreting Temperature Profiles..............145
    Brian Rozdilsky

In Process Oven Temperature Monitoring Application to
Porcelain Enamel Firing...153
    Steve Offley

Furnace Efficiency..165
    Kevin Coursin

Recent and Developing Environmental Rules and Policies
Impacting Manufacturing..169
    Jack Waggener

General Concepts for the Production of Enameling Steel......175
    Robert Yap

Preface

The Porcelain Enamel Institute Technical Forum committee is pleased to present the Proceedings of the 2013 Technical Forum held in Nashville in May 2013. Many thanks go out to those in the industry who gave extra time out of their busy jobs to give papers at the Tech Forum (and even more to those who follow up with written papers!). Thanks also go out to the committee for planning the Tech Forum, and to the Back-to-Basics faculty who, as always, did an excellent job doing a one day training seminar on porcelain enamels the day before the Tech Forum.

The 2013 Proceedings covered a wide range of topics such as the mechanical properties of enamel, flow coating internal water heater coils, the design of a state-of-the-art powder room, raw material trends, and temperature profiles within furnaces. The participants certainly left with a broader knowledge of enamel. This book documenting the technical presentations will no doubt be referred to by many enamellers, as the other volumes of the proceedings have been since 1937.

While much effort is made to document the knowledge presented at the Technical Forum in this book, there is even much more obtained by attending the Technical Forum. The 2013 Forum started off with an arm chair discussion of the industry with Silvano Pagliuca (International Enameling Institute), Ken Kaluzny (Coral Chemical), Glenn Pfendt (AO Smith), Mike Cukier (Whirlpool), and Ben Stephen (Weber). Topics covered included new applications for porcelain enamel, consumer trends, barriers that prevent adoption of enamel, and opportunities to improve the enameling process. Additionally, there are many face-to-face meetings at Suppliers Mart, the chance to ask experts questions, and much training, particularly Back-to-Basics.

As this Proceedings goes to print, the Technical Forum committee is busy working on the 2014 Tech Forum to be held in Nashville with more new information for the enameller to benefit our industry. We look forward to a successful meeting of the industry there. We are also looking forward to the 2015 International Enameling Congress in at the Convitto della Calza in Florence, Italy. The Convitto della Calza is located in the heart of the city, unique among Florence hotels for its combination of a 16th-century cloister and halls frescoed with masterpieces such as Francibigio's Last Supper, with very modern meeting rooms and hospitality in a charming location. A full program is planned with two days of technical presentations and two days of plant visits.

Charles Baldwin
Ferro Corporation
Tech Forum Proceedings Editor

2013 PEI Officers

Chairman of the Board
JACK WAGGENER
URS Corporation

President
KEVIN COURSIN
KMI Systems, Inc.

Vice Presidents

BOB ANDERSON
EIC Group North America

PETER DORITY
Coral Chemical Company

LIAM O'BYRNE
West Coast Porcelain

GLENN PFENDT
A O Smith Corporation

BRYAN STOCKDALE
WinsorFireform

DAVE THOMAS
Pemco Corporation

DEBRA VOGES
Roesch, Inc.

Executive Committee Members
JONATHAN DAVIES
Pemco Corporation

WILLIAM GANZER
Mapes and Sprowl Steel

MIKE HORTON
KMI Systems, Inc.

DON McCORMICK
Electrolux Home Products

PETER VODAK
A O Smith Corporation

MILES VOTAVA
Ferro Corporation

Treasurer
PHIL FLASHER
Gema USA

Executive Vice President
CULLEN HACKLER
PEI

2013 TECHNICAL FORUM COMMITTEE

Chairman: Ben Stephen (Weber-Stephen Products)
Vice Chairman: David Latimer (Whirlpool Corporation)

Charles Baldwin (Ferro Corporation)
Jeff Dailidas (Nordson Corporation)
Peter Dority (Coral Chemical Company)
Holger Evele (Ferro Corporation)
Phil Flasher (Gema USA)
Cullen Hackler (Porcelain Enamel Institute)
Mike Horton (KMI Systems, Inc.)
Joe Melaro (A O Smith Protective Coatings)
Liam O'Byrne (O'Byrne Consulting Services)
Dave Thomas (Pemco Corporation)
Peter Vodak (A O Smith Corporation)
Miles Votava (Ferro Corporation)
Jack Waggener (URS Corporation)
Ted Wolowicz (Electrolux Home Products)
Jeff Wright (Ferro Corporation)

Porcelain Enamel Institute, Inc.
PO Box 920220
Norcross, GA 30010
Phone: 770-676-9366
Fax: 770-409-7280
E-mail: penamel@aol.com
www.buyporcelain.org
www.porcelainenamel.com

PAST CHAIRS OF PEI TECHNICAL FORUMS

Ben Stephen...2012-13
   Weber-Stephen Products Company
Mike Horton..2010-11
   KMI Systems, Inc.
Peter Vodak..2008-09
   A O Smith Corporation
Holger Evele...2006-07
   Ferro Corporation
Steve Kilczewski...2004-05
   Pemco Corporation
Liam O'Byrne..2002-03
   AB&I Foundry
Jeff Sellins..2000-01
   Maytag Cooking Products
Robert Reese...1998-99
   Frigidaire Home Products
David Thomas...1996-97
   The Erie Ceramic Arts Company
Rusty Rarey..1994-95
   LTV Steel Company
Douglas Giese...1992-93
   GE Appliances
Anthony Mazzuca..1990-91
   Mobay Corporation
William McClure..1988-89
   Magic Chef
Larry Steele..1986-87
   Armco Steel
Donald Sauder..1984-85
   WCI-Range Division
James Quigley...1982-83
   Ferro Corporation
George Hughes...1980-81
   Vitreous Steel Products Company
Lester Smith...1978-79
   Porcelain Metals Corporation
Evan Oliver...1977
   Bethlehem Steel Corporation
Wayne Gasper..1975-76
   The Maytag Company
Donald Toland..1973-74
   U.S. Steel Corporation
Archie Farr..1971-72
   O. Hommel Company

Harold Wilson...1969-70
  Vitreous Steel Products Company
Forrest Nelson..1967-68
  A.O. Smith Corporation

Grant Miller..1965-66
  Ferro Corporation
Mel Gibbs...1963-64
  Inland Steel Company
Charles Kleinhans...1961-62
  Porcelain Metals Corporation
James Willis..1959-60
  Pemco Corporation
Lewis Farrow..1957-58
  Whirlpool Corporation
Gene Howe...1955-56
  Chicago Vitreous Corporation
W.H. "Red" Pfieffer...1953-54
  Frigidaire Division, G.M.C.
Roger Fellows...1951-52
  Chicago Vitreous Corporation
Glenn McIntyre..1948-50
  Ferro Corporation
Frank Hodek...1936-47
  General Porcelain Enameling and Mfg. Company

Fracture Analysis of Laminate Porcelain Enamel Coatings

Bradley Potter
Case Western Reserve University
Department of Materials Science and Engineering

Kyla McKinley, Charles Baldwin
Ferro Corporation

Fracture of bi-layer porcelain enamel coatings on a steel substrate was analyzed using torsion testing at room temperature. The design of experiment was based on previous work performed by the Ferro Corporation. Results of the testing confirmed the theory that the three primary variables affecting coating durability were the difference in thermal expansion coefficient between the enamel and steel, the Young's Modulus of the enamel, and the thickness of the coating. A larger difference in thermal expansion results in a greater compressive stress in the coating, which makes the coating stronger. A thicker coating is weaker, although the precise reason for this is uncertain. The influence of the Young's Modulus is the most complex, as a larger modulus inherently lends itself to a stronger coating and a larger residual compressive stress, but a smaller modulus corresponds to a less stiff coating which can bend more before failure. Data suggests that the flexibility of the coating predominates, with a lower modulus giving a more durable coating.

Introduction

Ferro Corporation (Ferro from here forward) manufactures glass frit and milled glass powders which are used in manufacturing to create porcelain enamel glass coatings on a wide variety of products including cookware, plumbing, water heaters, and industrial equipment. The coatings are used for their high-temperature characteristics, as well as their hard, abrasion-resistant mechanical properties. However, the coatings are brittle and fail in tension, causing crazing, cracking, and spallation of the coating off of the base metal. Acquiring a deeper understanding of this failure can help change the design and testing practices used to develop and manufacture enamels, adding value to Ferro's products and services and helping save customers' time and money. Information learned through this research is also of interest to the Porcelain Enamel Institute as a way of enhancing the fundamental understanding of glasses and composite coatings, applicable to other related research and industrial applications.

Prior work has been performed at Ferro by Charles Baldwin, Holger Evele, and Kyla McKinley to study the fracture of porcelain enamel coatings[1]. Their study laid the groundwork for this current study, but the material selection has been altered slightly in order to reduce the influence of confounding variables. The results of Ferro's prior study contradicted theory regarding the strength of the coatings, so this study was arranged as a follow-up to either confirm the theory or confirm the previous results and disprove the theory. The current study has three main components:

1) Repeat the design of experiment (DOE) with a different selection of materials to collect new coating durability data. Compare findings with theory.
2) Perform a literature review to confirm or refute the existing theory of coating durability.
3) Use findings to improve the testing and design process for new enamel coatings. Ideally a model will be developed allowing for accurate computer simulation of coating characteristics allowing for coating optimization.

Background

Like most brittle materials, porcelain enamels are strong in compression but weak in tension. Therefore, failure is expected to occur in the direction of greatest tensile load on the coating. Theoretically, the simplest way to increase the strength of the coating is to process the sample in such a way that the residual compressive stress on the enamel is maximized so when a tensile load is applied it must first overcome the compressive stress before it can cause tensile failure in the enamel. During the processing of the coating, the milled powder enamel is applied to the surface of the metal and then fired at high temperature to allow for the glass to flow and form a cohesive coating layer before cooling through the glass transition temperature to become rigid once again. Due to the large fluctuations in temperature during this process, the materials expand and contract, and the difference between the coefficient of thermal expansion (CTE) of the metal and the enamel results in a residual compressive stress in the enamel according to the following Equation 1:

$$\sigma_c = \frac{E_e(\alpha_e - \alpha_s)(\Delta T)}{\frac{t_e}{t_s} * \frac{E_e}{E_s} + 1} \quad \text{(Eq. 1)}$$

where is the residual compressive stress in the enamel, E is the Young's modulus of the enamel, is the CTE, is the temperature drop during which the residual stress forms, t is the layer thickness, e indicates a property of the enamel, and s indicates a property of the steel. Under the assumption that residual compressive stress dictates the strength of the coating, equation 1 dictates the key relationships. A larger difference in CTE will lead to a stronger coating, and since steel has a larger CTE than most enamels, generally the smaller the CTE of the enamel the stronger the coating. The drop from the glass temperature on cooling is assumed to be essentially the same for all coatings since the firing temperatures have minimal variation. This equation suggests that the thicker the coating is, the weaker it will be for a given steel thickness. It is not immediately clear how the Young's modulus will influence the strength, though the modulus in the numerator will likely dominate, suggesting a larger modulus will produce a stronger coating.

The theoretical strength of glasses is never reached in practice because of the presence of flaws in materials. For very small nano- or micro-scale materials, there will be a lower probability of the sample containing a defect that would initiate failure. However, for macro-scale samples there will always be defects that concentrate stresses and induce failure at stresses far below the theoretical strength of the material. This is the basis of the Griffith theory of failure. According to Griffith's theory, the critical stress at failure can be found using Equation 2:

$$\sigma_f = \sqrt{\frac{2E\gamma}{\pi c}} \quad \text{(Eq. 2)}^2$$

where is the stress at failure, E is the Young's Modulus, is the specific surface energy, and c is half of the crack length. Based on equation 2, an increase in Young's Modulus should correspond to a stronger coating, as predicted above from equation 1.

Based on these equations, it appears that the most significant variables influencing the strength of a coating are the CTE, the Young's Modulus, and the coating thickness. Using push-rod dilatometry, it is possible to measure the CTE of materials, including both the substrate metal and the ceramics used for coating. Thickness of the coating is controlled by the application rate of the coating to the surface during processing prior to firing. Thickness is also measured easily with a handheld unit. However, the Modulus of glasses with complex chemistries is difficult to predict and difficult to measure. It is desirable to have a theoretical approach for predicting the modulus of a glass based on its chemistry, and also an experimental method to confirm the accuracy of the theory. One technique used to theoretically predict the elastic constant of a glass was proposed by Makishima and Mackenzie[3] based on theory used for ionic crystals[4]. The expression derived is Equation 3:

$$E = 83.6 * V \sum(G * X) \quad \text{(Eq. 3)}$$

where V is a packing density factor, G is the dissociation energy per unit volume of each oxide component, and X is the mole fraction of each component. While apparently straightforward, there are a few problems with applying this equation to the enamel coatings. First, the parameters, especially the dissociation energy of each component, are very difficult to find tabulated anywhere, making it difficult to employ in practice. Second, application of this model to borate glasses adds complexity because there are both 3- and 4-coordinated boron atoms present which have to be accounted for with an empirical ratio of the number of each state present.[4]

A second method has been developed by Yamane and Sakaino[5] that is simpler to apply and that avoids the complexity of borates. This approach uses the melting point of each individual component as an indicator of its intermolecular bonding strength. This is shown in Equation 4:

$$E = \frac{0.0093*\rho}{M} * \Sigma(T_{m,i} * X_i) \text{ (Eq. 4)}$$

where is the overall density of the glass in g/cc, M is the average molecular weight of the glass in g/mol, is the melting point of each component in Kelvin, and is the mole fraction of each component. The density of the glass is easy to measure, and the melting point and molar mass of each component is readily available. Therefore, for a glass of known composition, the Young's Modulus can be approximated easily. Comparison of the Sakaino approximation to empirical data for several known moduli showed less than 5% error[6].

In addition to theoretical calculations, an experimental technique is desired to validate the modulus of glasses as needed. Due to the high theoretical modulus and strength of glasses and the equipment needed to perform accurate testing, performing standard tensile bar testing is not a practical approach. Microhardness of a sample can be measured and correlated to a modulus value, but this approach is still a rather rough approximation. Based on research, the most widely accepted method for measuring Young's Modulus is based on sonic resonance of cylindrical or rectangular bars. There are two applicable standards from ASTM, methods C1198 and E1875[7,8]. These methods as applied to glasses are identical, involving mechanically inducing a wave from one end of a sample and measuring the response of the wave on the other end of the sample. The procedures also outline a way of performing the test at elevated temperatures, so the Modulus can be measured relative to temperature. Ultimately, Equation 5 is used to determine the Young's Modulus of a cylindrical sample:

$$E = 1.6067 * \frac{L^3}{D^4} * m * f^2 * CF \quad (Eq. 5)$$

L is the length of the specimen, D is the diameter of the specimen, m is the mass of the specimen, f is the measured frequency, and CF is a correction factor that is defined in detail in the ASTM standards. The testing equipment needed to perform this test is quite specialized, so a testing lab with the equipment needs to be found or the equipment can be purchased for in-house testing.

Procedure

The same steel was used for all testing, provided by Whirlpool in Clyde, Ohio. Sheets of A424 Type I steel arrived and were cut into strips approximately 12" x 2". Holes were punched into one end of the strip and each strip was bent 90 degrees along its long axis to form two 12" x 1" faces. Each steel sample had to be cleaned with a ground coat slip to remove any rust or oils from the surface, maximizing adhesion of the coating. An electrostatic dry-spray process was used to apply a uniform 6 to 7 gram coating of ground coat powder on both the convex and concave sides of the sample. Each sample was hung on a hook and fired at the specified temperature for 3.5 minutes in the hot zone. Once cool, a 6 to

7 gram layer of cover coat was applied via wet spray application on the convex surface only. The wet layer had to dry completely, and then a protective cover was placed on the center of the convex surface and a paintbrush was used to wipe away the dried cover coat around the edges of the surface. The sample was again hung on a hook and fired at the same temperature as the ground coat for 3.5 minutes. At this point the ground coat and cover coat are both fully developed and the sample should look like the diagram in Figure 1.

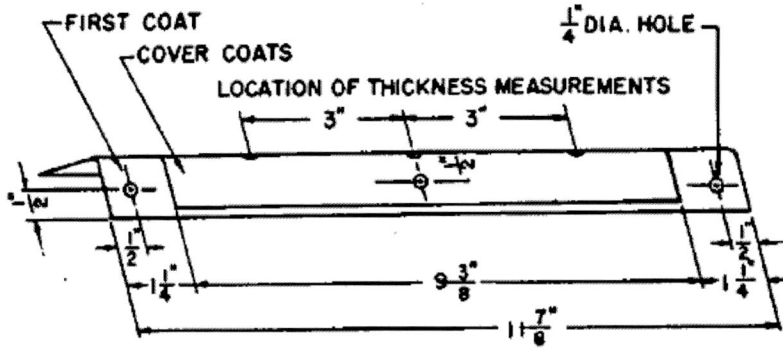

Figure 1. Torsion bar geometry

Before torsion testing could be performed, the thickness of the enamel coating had to be measured at three equidistant points along the convex surface of the sample, as indicated in Figure 1. With the sample prepared and the coating thickness measured, the bar was placed in the torsion testing device shown in Figure 2, which held one end of the sample fixed while rotating the other end at a rate of 100 degrees per minute. Failure was identified by visual inspection during testing. The test was stopped when spalling began and the angle was measured.

Figure 2. Torsion testing equipment

The materials selected for testing for both the original lab work and the follow up lab work are outlined in Tables 1, 2, 3, and 4 below. The original cover coat materials selected (C and D) were novel coating materials developed by Ferro; the second set of cover coats (E and F) were selected because of their very similar chemistry and therefore the belief that they should have similar moduli.

Enamel	CTE (1/°C)	Glass Transition (°F)
A	$10.1 * 10^{-6}$	833
B	$8.9 * 10^{-6}$	907

Table 1. Properties of ground coat

Enamel	CTE (1/°C)	Glass Transition (°F)
C	$11.2 * 10^{-6}$	768
D	$9.0 * 10^{-6}$	881

Table 2. Properties of cover coats used in original testing

Enamel	CTE (1/°C)	Glass Transition (°F)
E	$11.01 * 10^{-6}$	824
F	$8.61 * 10^{-6}$	892

Table 3. Properties of cover coats used in current testing

CTE (1/°C)
$12.1 * 10^{-6}$

Table 4. Property of steel

Three samples were selected after torsion testing for microstructural analysis. To enhance the cross sectional area of the coatings, the samples were cut to reveal a standard cross section, but during polishing the samples were fixed to polish at a 30 degree angle to the torsion bars' surface, thus doubling the cross sectional area. Samples were inspected using a digital camera and stereoscope at 25 and 50 times magnification.

In order to perform the Young's Modulus theoretical calculations, the density of the glass had to be determined. In order to perform these calculations, samples of the glass frit were placed in a beaker of water with a scale, measuring their volume and mass so that the density could be calculated. The arrangement used for this density measurement is shown below in Figure 3.

Figure 3. Apparatus used to measure density

Previous Results

During the first set of testing, samples were prepared with combinations of ground coats A and B, cover coats C and D, and firing temperatures of 1500 and 1540°F. These combinations are indicated in the legend in Figure 4, which plots the torsion angle at failure versus the thickness of the coatings. Each point on the plot represents 5 data points, an average of the 5 thinnest and 5 thickest coatings at each testing condition. A total of 10 samples were tested for each set of testing conditions. One set was run with a 1-to-1 mixture of the ground coats and 1-to-1 mixture of the cover coats, each prepared by mixing equal parts of the milled powders prior to spraying and firing the samples. This specimen was also run at 1520°F.

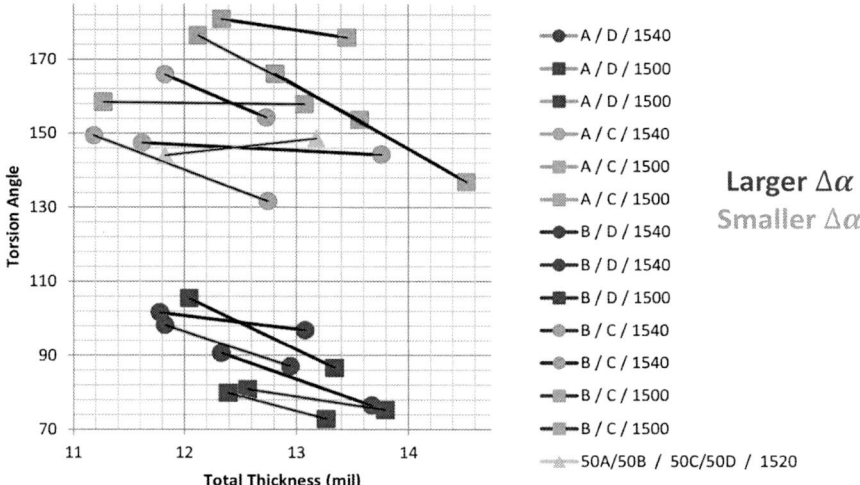

Figure 4. Results of previous Ferro testing. The larger difference in CTE between steel and cover coat exists for the red points.

Results

The same testing was performed in the new design of experiment, except that the cover coats C and D were replaced with cover coats E and F, respectively. The data which resulted can be seen in Figure 6 on the next page.

Bubble structure images were taken of three samples. These images are provided in Figure 5.

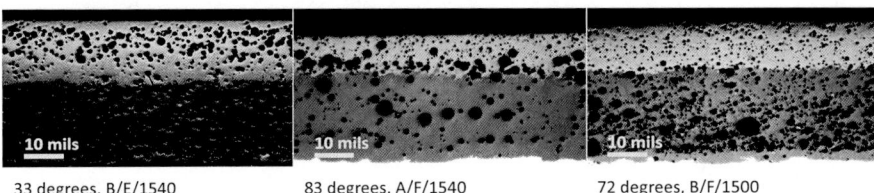

33 degrees, B/E/1540   83 degrees, A/F/1540   72 degrees, B/F/1500

Figure 5. Bubble structure images of three samples. The captions indicate the "Failure Angle, Ground Coat / Cover Coat / Firing Temperature" of the three samples.

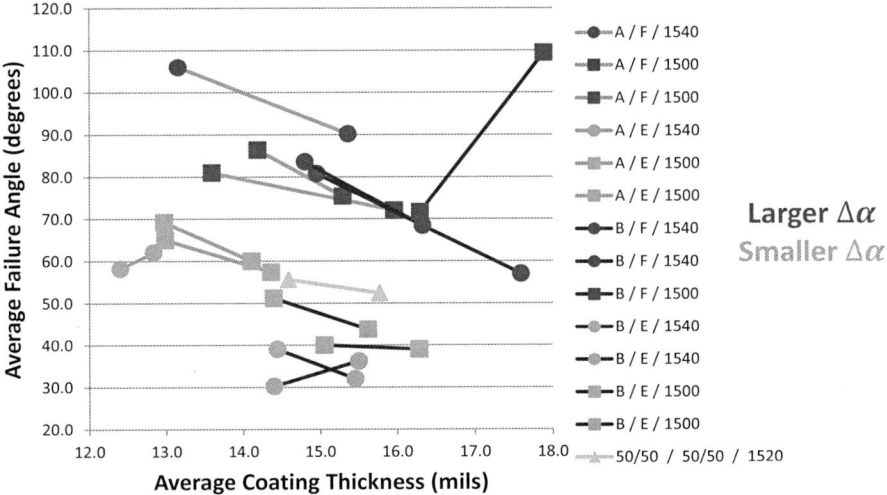

Figure 6. Results of the current testing. The larger difference in CTE between steel and cover coat exists for the red points.

The fracture surfaces of several samples were imaged from an overhead perspective. These images are shown in Figure 7 below.

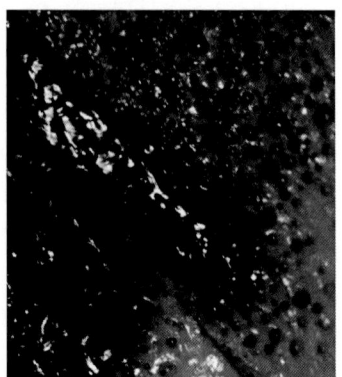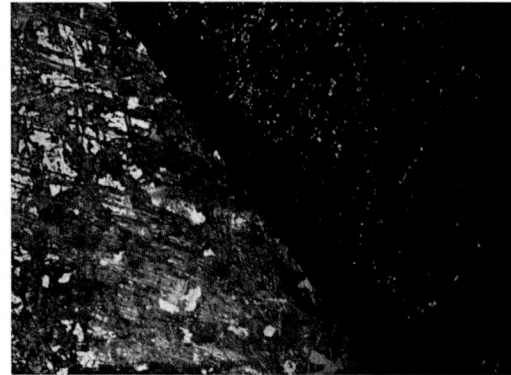

Figure 7. Overhead fracture surface images at 50x magnification. Lighter colored material is the cover coat, dark grey material is the exposed ground coat.

All four cover coats used between the two studies were analyzed using the Sakaino method to determine the theoretical Young's Modulus. The resulting moduli are provided in Table 5 below, along with the measured density needed to calculate the modulus.

Cover Coat	C	D	E	F
ρ (g/cc)	2.89	2.68	2.69	2.67
E (GPa)	43.4	58.0	56.9	61.2

Table 5. Theoretical Young's Modulus calculations for cover coats

Additional samples beyond the requirements of the primary DOE underwent torsion testing using an Instron machine with a load cell so that the applied load could be measured during the test. The resulting load versus angle plot is provided in Figure 8 below.

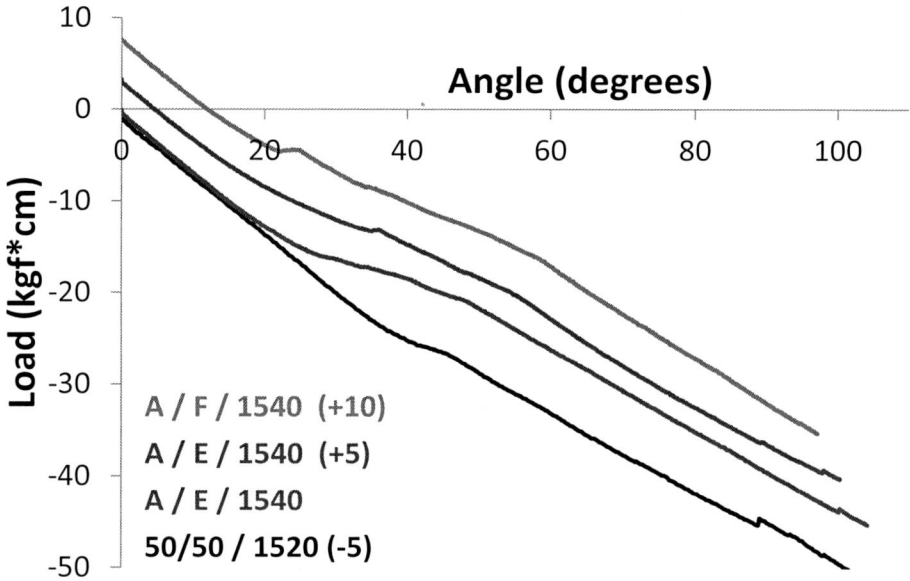

Figure 8. Load versus angle data for samples tested using Instron. The lines were offset by 5 kgf*cm each so that the details could be seen, as indicated by the (+10), (+5), and (-5) in the legend. "Ground Coat / Cover Coat / Firing Temperature (offset)" is provided for each curve.

Discussion

Figure 4 showing the results of Ferro's previous study clearly indicates that the cover coat with the larger difference in CTE relative to the steel (cover coat D) ended up being the weaker coating. This contradicts what the theory outlined in Equation 1 suggests. The coatings did get weaker as coating thickness increased, which aligns with the theoretical interpretation. It was this unexpected result with regards to the CTE that prompted a second study. Pareto analysis performed by Ferro suggested that the cover coat exhibited the strongest correlation to coating strength, so it was the cover coat that was analyzed further in the second set of tests.

When materials were selected for the cover coats for the recent trial, two coatings with very similar chemistries were selected to eliminate some potential confounding variables from the first set of tests. The only significant difference between coatings was believed to be the CTE, where cover coat E had a CTE nearly as large as the steel while cover coat F had a much lower CTE than the steel. Based on this information, theory suggested that cover coat F should be stronger. As seen in Figure 6, this was the case. Cover coat F with a much larger difference in CTE failed at a significantly higher torsion angle than cover coat E. Once again there was a decrease in coating strength with increasing coating thickness, as predicted in Equation 1. The noteworthy deviation from the trend of decreasing strength with increasing thickness was seen at the top right corner of Figure 6. One point exhibited very high strength despite having the thickest average coating. The most likely explanation for this is that these specimens had very few bubbles. Since bubbles would act as cracks in Equation 2, if a coating was present with very few large bubbles to act as stress concentrators, then the sample would exhibit an unusually high strength.

In addition to the mathematical explanation provided by Equation 1, there are several qualitative explanations regarding why an increase in coating thickness may correspond to a weaker coating. First, a thicker coating would cool slightly slower than a thin coating. While the enamel is cooling but is still above the glass transition temperature, the glass would still be able to flow and relieve some of the residual stresses, thus reducing the residual stress present in the coating when it reaches room temperature. With less residual stress, the coating will fail in tension under a smaller applied load. Second, the surface of a thick coating will be slightly farther from the axis of rotation during the torsion testing. As a result, when the sample undergoes a given angular rotation, the linear strain experienced by the cover coat will be slightly larger than for a thinner coating. Lastly, as suggested by the Griffith

Theory of fracture mechanics, the more material that is present, the greater the probability of a large flaw existing somewhere in the coating that will concentrate the stress and cause failure at a low applied stress. As the coating gets thicker, there is more material to potentially trap bubbles or other defects, translating to failure at lower stresses and torsion angles. These factors may contribute to the weakening of the coating as coating thickness increases.

The most interesting result is the influence of the Young's Modulus of each cover coat. Coats E and F used in the current tests have only a small difference in moduli, so that the performance of the coating is controlled predominately by the difference in CTE between the cover coat and steel. Therefore, the larger difference in CTE leads to a larger residual compressive stress and the coating fails at a larger torsion angle. Cover coat D from the original test had a Young's Modulus close to E and F from the current testing. However, cover coat C had a significantly different chemistry which has a much lower Young's Modulus. Based on the theory of residual compressive stress and Griffith's Theory (Equations 1 and 2), the lower modulus should result in a weaker coating. However, the data shows distinctly the opposite result. Coat C with a small difference in CTE and by far the smallest modulus failed at a substantially larger angle than any other samples tested. This phenomenon is surprising at first, but the real problem here may be a flaw in the testing method. While the coating itself should have a lower strength and lower residual stress, the torsion test does not measure the load or stress applied to the sample. It only measures the torsion angle, or essentially the strain on the material. Therefore, a sample with a low modulus of elasticity essentially has a very low stiffness, meaning that the ratio of stress over strain is very low—the sample can rotate and bend a significant amount even at relatively low applied stress. Since the test as it is defined measures the strain (as torsion angle) and not the actual applied load or stress, a sample that is weak and flexible will appear strong, while a sample that is extremely strong and stiff may appear weak because it will fail at an extremely small torsion angle (despite a very large applied stress). Ultimately this means that the torsion testing without a load cell to measure the applied stress will not be a very accurate indicator of coating strength unless the coatings being compared have similar Young's Moduli.

With only three images, a relationship between bubble structure and coatings or firing temperatures cannot be identified. However, as the image on the left of Figure 7 shows, the failure in the coating clearly occurs along the bubble structure of the material. This agrees with the Griffith concept where failure occurs due to stress concentrators—the bubbles concentrate the stress and fracture occurs through the bubbles. As the cracks develop in the surface of the material perpendicular to the applied tensile load (at a 45 degree angle to the torsion axis), cracks propagate down from the cover coat and air interface and get deflected away from the steel. As these cracks meet throughout the sample the coating spalls off in slivers and chips, leaving distinct lines as shown by the image on the right of Figure 7.

Attempts were made to validate the theoretical Young's Modulus calculations with empirical data. The sonic resonance equipment described in ASTM C1198 and E1875 is not available on Case Western Reserve University campus or in the labs at Ferro. Work requests were submitted to Stork Herron Testing Labs and NSL Analytical in the Cleveland area, but neither lab had the sonic resonance equipment. No experimental data has been collected to validate the calculations in Table 5, although using the Sakaino method to calculate the theoretical moduli of known samples from the CES EduPack material database, less than 5% error was found, suggesting that the calculated moduli are relatively accurate.

Looking at the load cell results from Figure 8, one can see that in some cases a clear jump in the applied load occurred. Around 90 degrees on the black line, a jump is clearly visible. Similarly a jump in the load is visible around 100 degrees on the purple line. However, some of the data were not so clear; the blue line on the top of the graph shows no identifiable jump in the load, despite the coating having failed. The underlying principle for this approach is that when the cracks in the enamel grow and then the coating spalls off, energy is released. With this release in energy, the load required to continue twisting the sample temporarily drops. When this drop is large enough to be measured by the load cell, testing can be successfully automated so that the Instron identifies the jump in applied load as failure of the sample and stops the test automatically. However, when the enamel spalls off in very small pieces, the associated energy release is also very small, making the failure of the sample impossible to identify using the load versus angle plot. Due to this uncertainty, the load cell approach cannot run as an automated test. However the load cell data may be useful in further analysis of the system since (as mentioned above) the torsion angle alone can misrepresent the true strength and durability of the coating.

Conclusions

Based on the torsion testing performed during the most recent DOE and the theoretical Young's Modulus measurements, the relationship between coating strength and CTE or thickness is accurately represented by Equation 1, using the residual compressive stress as an indicator of strength. However, when the Young's Modulus varies significantly between coatings the torsion angle at failure becomes more difficult to predict. While the residual compressive stress increases with increasing Young's Modulus, so too does the stiffness of the coating. Therefore the applied load at failure should increase with a larger modulus, but since the torsion test measures strain and not stress, the torsion angle at failure may decrease with increasing modulus. The best way to account for the Young's Modulus would be to use a load cell to accurately measure both the stress and the strain during torsion.

As predicted by Griffith's Theory in equation 2, bubbles appear to act as stress concentrators and serve as initiation points for failure and the path along which cracks propagate through the enamel.

Lastly, the Sakaino method appears to provide an accurate approximation of the Young's Modulus of a glass with known composition. Empirical data found using sonic resonance testing can be used to validate these calculations.

Ultimately, the validity of the test depends on the stresses and strains that the enamel coatings undergo in the field. If there is typically a fixed strain or rotation of equipment during transportation and use, then the torsion test measuring failure angle is an appropriate test, and design of new enamels should try to maximize the difference in CTE between base metal and coating materials while minimizing coating thickness and the Young's Modulus within the constraints of the application. If a fixed stress is a more realistic approximation of the applications of enamel coatings, then the current testing procedure needs to be refined to incorporate a stress or load measurement in addition to the strain; the difference in CTE should still be maximized and the coating thickness minimized, but for a fixed load, a large modulus will translate to a more durable coating with minimal strain.

Acknowledgements

The authors would like to thank Ferro for supporting this project and working with Case Western Reserve University.

Dr. Mark De Guire served as the project adviser at Case Western, helping with any logistical concerns and providing some very useful technical input. He was also eager to answer my questions and his enthusiasm for my work was greatly appreciated.

Dr. John Lewandowski provided additional support as the class adviser and helped arrange lab time within the department, as well as providing occasional feedback on my progress.

Dr. Zhu and Chris Tuma were very helpful in performing lab work on campus at Case Western, providing the lab space, the equipment, and the training to take stereoscope images and perform Instron testing, respectively.

References

[1] Baldwin, Charles, Kyla McKinley, and Holger Evele. "Analysis of Fracture in Porcelain Enamels." *Proc. PEI Tech Forum* 74, (2012), pp. 53-70.

[2] Callister, William D, Jr., and David G Rethwisch. <u>Fundamentals of Materials Science and Engineering: An Integrated Approach.</u> Third Edition. 2008, John Wiley & Sons.

[3] Makishima, A, and J D Mackenzie. "Direct Calculation of Young's Modulus of Glass." <u>Journal of Non-Crystalline Solids,</u> 1973 (12). North-Holland Publishing Company.

[4] Kreidl, N J. <u>Glass: Science and Technology.</u> Edited by D R Uhlmann. Vol 5. 1980, Academic Press.

[5] Yamane, Masayuki, and Teruo Sakaino. "Calculation of Young's Modulus of Glass from its Chemical Composition and Density." <u>Glass Technology,</u> Vol 15, 5. October 1974.

[6] CES EduPack 2012. Granta Material Inspiration.

[7] "Standard Test Method for Dynamic Young's Modulus, Shear Modulus, and Poisson's Ratio for Advanced Ceramics by Sonic Resonance." Annual Book of ASTM Standards, 15.01, pg 253; 2007.

[8] "Standard Test Method for Dynamic Young's Modulus, Shear Modulus, and Poisson's Ratio by Sonic Resonance." Annual Book of ASTM Standards, 3.01, pg 1174; 2007.

Characterization of Electrostatic Enamel Powders: Study of Flow Properties Using Innovative Measurement Methodology

Pascal Delbaere, Johan De Soete
Pemco International

The enameling industry relies on highly streamlined and automated production processes such as porcelain powder coating to obtain their objectives because of the combined effects of the soft global economic picture and advances in technology. Technical installation parameters and specifications of the materials used are defined and matched as precisely as possible. A measurement methodology to characterize the enamel powder that is meaningful and relevant to the process is therefore absolutely necessary.

Introduction

In the broadest sense, powders are defined as an assembly of fine solid particles which interact with each other. Powders typically have a very large specific surface area and, as a result of the amount of lattice defects present on the surface of the individual powder particles, they exhibit a high surface energy (activity). Because of these characteristics, powders are particularly suitable for use in process technology.

The physical properties of the particles (e.g., size, shape, surface texture, hardness, and chemical reactivity) affect the interactions between the individual particles and, therefore, the processing properties of a powder. Furthermore, particles are surrounded by fluid and gas (usually air); this external parameter largely determines the powder behavior.

Because the ratio between these components (e.g. the influence of humidity) can be so variable, these materials are difficult to characterize and their behavior is often unpredictable in terms of workability. One can describe flow ability as the ease with which a material can be made to flow. After this simple definition powder flow ability is a one-dimensional characteristic so powders are classified on a sliding scale ranging from "free flowing" to "non-flowing". Flow behavior of a powder is by no means an inherent material property, but is a function of the physical material properties influencing the powder flow as well as powder treatment, storage, and processing. When describing flow behavior the effects of external factors such as humidity, temperature, and especially the packing state cannot be emphasized enough; powder in an aerated state (e.g. in a fluidized bed) behaves as a liquid and in the compacted state (e.g. tablet, briquette) as a solid. Unfortunately, during processing generally the actual powder state is situated between these extremes. Therefore, a more precise definition of powder flow ability is the ability of a powder to flow in a desired way in a specific device.

In powder technology, typical terms that are used to express flow behavior of a powder are: bulk density, permeability, cohesion, fluidity and wall friction. These 'variables' arise from the collective forces such as van der Waals, electrostatic forces, surface tension, particle interlocking, friction, etc., which act on individual particles. Basically consideration of the inter-particle forces should allow a good description of the behavior of a powder. Because a technical powder is composed of particles of different type, physical state and size, we quickly end up with a complex multi-component system, which can lead to diverse effects.

In contrast to traditional "single number" methods that are often criticized for their lack of reproducibility, the newest methods try to describe flow behavior in a more comprehensive way that is relevant to the process. Forces and deformations on a defined and conditioned volume are measured. Investigations showed that dynamic characterization techniques are best suited to predict the fluidization behavior, while the more static techniques are better suited to determine the cohesivity of a powder. In other words, both static and dynamic characterization techniques are necessary to fully understand the flow behavior of a powder and to be able to predict how the material will behave under different process conditions.

Electrostatic Powder Application and Powder Characterization

The high performance and low environmental impact of electrostatically applied powder enamels make them attractive for a variety of applications. The powder flowing easily and smoothly through the powder application system is very important to reproduce consistent quality results. Furthermore a steady powder flow during the manufacturing of the powder-enamel can contribute to a quality improvement and/or a significant reduction in process time.

In the electrostatic powder coating process, the powder is carried then sprayed on the part by suspension in air. Early in the development of the technology, the company SAMES has designed a device to determine this behavior and to specify whether the powder is suitable for spraying or not. It remains a valuable tool for both the powder manufacturer and the applicator. Still, in the context of increased demands, certain phenomena remain unexplained and complex issues regarding flow ability stay unanswered based on these measurements. However, due to recent advances in measurement technology, a more effective understanding of the term "flow ability" is possible. Modern powder rheometers are better able to define how the powder should flow. Using a well-chosen simulation of the packing state, it becomes possible to characterize the flow behavior of enamel powder when stored, consolidated, forced to flow by applied pressure, aerated during transport, or fluidized in a container.

The FT4 Powder Rheometer from Freeman Technology was evaluated. This does not rule out that other instruments or measurement methodologies that may be equally well suited for this purpose. Because the data are calculated from a fully automatic force and torque measurement, calibration is possible, the operator influence is minimized and the reproducibility is obtained.

In the dynamic mode, which determines the energy needed to move a known volume of powder sample, the movement is controlled by a blade that rotates transversely through the powder sample and moves vertically along a well-defined helix. The measuring principle is based on the fundamentals of classical mechanics. According to Newton's First law, the forces responsible for the deformation and movement of the powder are proportional to the forces by which the blade is forced through the powder. The blade can be operated in different ways. The shape of the helix, speed and direction can be varied. On this basis, measurement protocols are set up in which the influence of repeated testing is measured (product stability) or in which the response to different conditioning states is investigated (compacted, aerated, etc.).

Case Study I: Product Development

The relationship between particle morphology and additives was studied. Flow ability is governed by inter-particle forces. For uncoated particles, due to the mechanical anchoring, a high energy (BFE) is required to move the powder. An overdose of additives leads to an increased cohesiveness; more energy is required to turn a sticky powder into motion. An optimal level of additives is derived at which the best flow characteristics are obtained. In product development the main focus is set on primary factors (e.g. particle size and shape, type and amount of coating additives). With an appropriate set of test parameters, secondary (external) variables, such as moisture content, degree of segregation and air content can be investigated in the same way.

Case Study II: Characterization of Installation Powder

A study was done to find process-relevant characterization of flow behavior of installation powders. An enamel-powder should be free flowing and readily aerated in the fluid reservoir, thereby ensuring that the individual particles are separated. The easier the powder flows through the spray gun, the better will be its electrostatic charging and the more uniform the coating. Powder that does not adhere to the substrate is recovered and brought back in circulation. Since the fine particles are more strongly influenced by the aerodynamic and electrostatic forces, an accumulation of very fine material during the process cannot be avoided. The fine particle size fraction is a critical parameter because it strongly affects fluidization, compaction and segregation. Regarding the importance for the process, it is not necessary to emphasize the need for a correct and process-relevant characterization of flow behavior of installation powders. Studies demonstrated that determination of flow energy (FE) on aerated samples is a reliable test to characterize powders for electrostatic application; important features are the first response to ventilation, the sharpness of the curve and the energy required to fluidize the material.

Because fine powders have a large surface area per mass unit, they are usually difficult to fluidize and when pumped they tend to travel in cohesive packages. The packages do not disintegrate when sprayed and cause uneven defected surfaces. FT4 measurements (FE - Aeration mode) have shown good correlation with the observations at the process line. Grain size measurements and determination of water content in the powder confirmed these findings. With the classical methods (e.g. Sames) it has been impossible to differentiate installation samples. Since modern powder rheometers enable us to write process-related protocols, we are able to classify samples from good to bad and consequently define a process window.

Case Study III: Plant Parameters and Powder Properties Matched

This was an attempt to closely match the processing properties of a test and reference material. Although a low cohesion and high fluidity is desirable, a level of cohesiveness can be advantageous to avoid segregation, attrition and dust generation. As such there is for every single powder/machine combination an optimal balance between cohesiveness and flow ability. The powder should behave in a stable manner during processing. The technical parameters of equipment and technical data of the powder should be perfectly matched to each other so that a maximum output is reached. This implies that a reliable prediction regarding the functioning of a product is necessary. With a targeted modification of parameters influencing flow behavior in our manufacturing process (DOE), an attempt was made to closely match the processing properties. Although improvement is certainly present, this approach has been evaluated positively in practice.

Conclusion

Powder behavior is very complex. As in every process, even in each process step, the powder is subjected to a specific set of parameters (bulk density, consolidation, etc.). The flow ability of a powder should always be considered and expressed in relation with the conditioning state. The powder properties should be as widely adapted to the process or vice versa. The use of state of the art measuring technology enables a controlled simulation of different powder conditioning states as well as an accurate measurement of their response to the imposed powder state. Typical flow properties of each powder product have been determined under laboratory conditions, and, this is expected to lead to a better understanding of the behavior of a powder, a more efficient product formulation and a higher final quality of the product.

Improving the Substrate Wettability of an Enamel Through the Use of a Surfactant

Joe Melaro and Laura Hughes
AO Smith Protective Coatings Division

Flow coating the inner diameter of water heater coils is a challenging enamel application requiring good process control in cleaning and flow coating, and can be improved by adding a surfactant to the enamel.

Enameling internal coils that are used inside hot water tanks like those shown in Figure 1 is a challenging problem. Application of the enamel to the interior and exterior of the coils is required.

Figure 1. Examples of internal tank coils

The steel surface on the interior of the coil can be difficult to enamel. The fired surface is shown in Figure 2 with copperheads or burn-off.

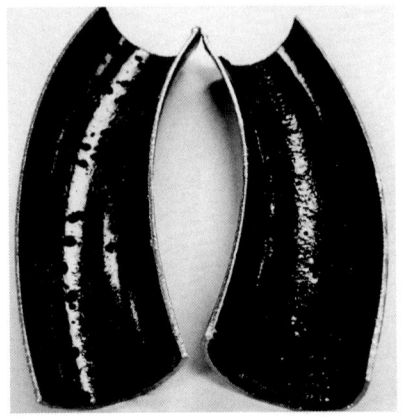 

Figure 2. Fired enamel surface on coil interior

The washing and enameling process shown in Figure 3 was investigated for the source of the defects.

(a) (b)

(c)　　　　　　　　　　　　(d)

Figure 3. (a) Cleaning and (b), (c) enamel application to coils, (d) drying

The process evaluation showed:

- Analysis with a borescope revealed that coil ID is 100% covered with dry bisque after drying and that enamel "crawls" only after firing.
- After drying, coils were fired in a different department's furnace – same "crawling" defect.
- Coils were hand-washed instead of going through the washer – no "crawling" defects.

Lab tests revealed that the alkaline cleaner the plant was using was an efficient cleaner and was not the problem. When a coil was cleaned with the plant's alkaline cleaner, there was no problem with coverage.

Further plant investigations revealed that the coil opening at the top did not always match up to the washer spray nozzles so the plant designed and installed guides so that the coil opening would meet up to the washer spray nozzles. The plant also added baffles at bottoms of some coils to provide back pressure to improve cleaner effectiveness. Both modifications are shown in Figure 4.

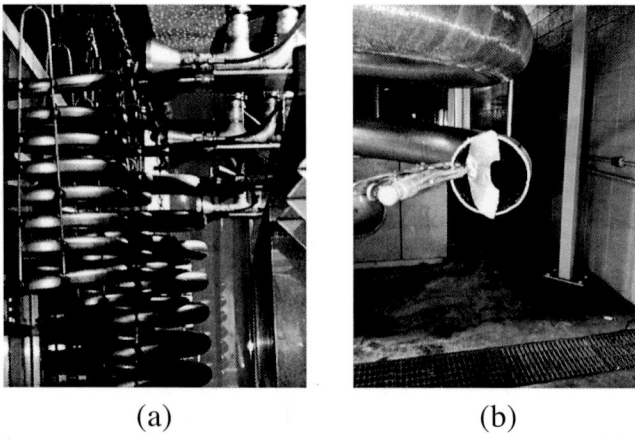

(a)   (b)

Figure 4. (a) Re-designed washer spray nozzle guides and (b) baffles

A surfactant was also added to the enamel to enhance enamel/substrate wettability while waiting for the guides to be made and installed. Surfactant is a contraction for "surface active agent." The characteristic molecular structure of such a compound is a water loving hydrophilic part and an oil loving ligophilic part. The surfactant reduces the surface tension to allow the enamel to wet out on any poorly cleaned internal section of the coil.

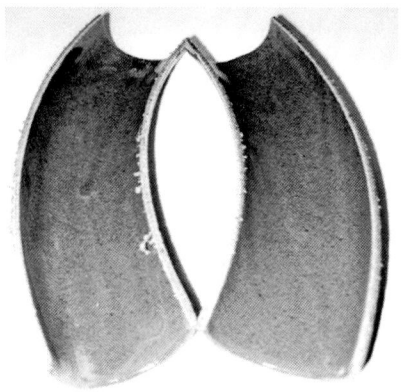 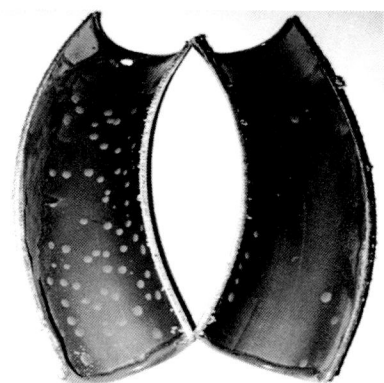

Surfactant A   Surfactant B

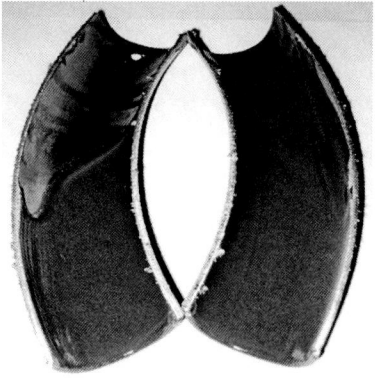 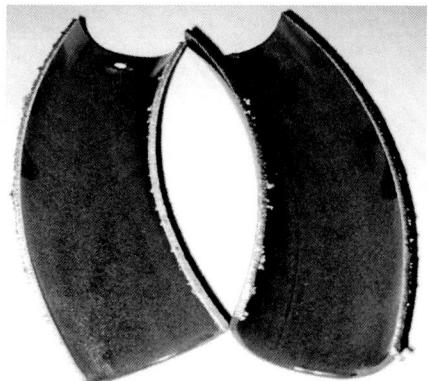

Surfactant C   Surfactant D

Figure 5. Results of surfactant testing

Figure 5 shows the results of testing four different surfactants. Surfactant A showed the best results for:

- Wetting out on the oily substrate the best.
- Producing a defect free and uniform enamel surface.
- Not causing foaming.
- Only a slight increase in enamel set that could be adjusted.

Combining the Best Technologies for Powder Porcelain Enamel Coating Applications

John Carlson
Nordson Corporation

State of the art application equipment such as Prodigy high density low volume (HDLV) technology and Encore guns with Venturi pumps have been chosen for porcelain and plant systems recently installed at new enameling plants. These systems deliver more powder while minimizing wasted air.

The powder application process in Figure 1 shows the control, powder pump, and spray gun options. Within the process, the powder consists of charged particles suspended in compressed air that behaves like a liquid.

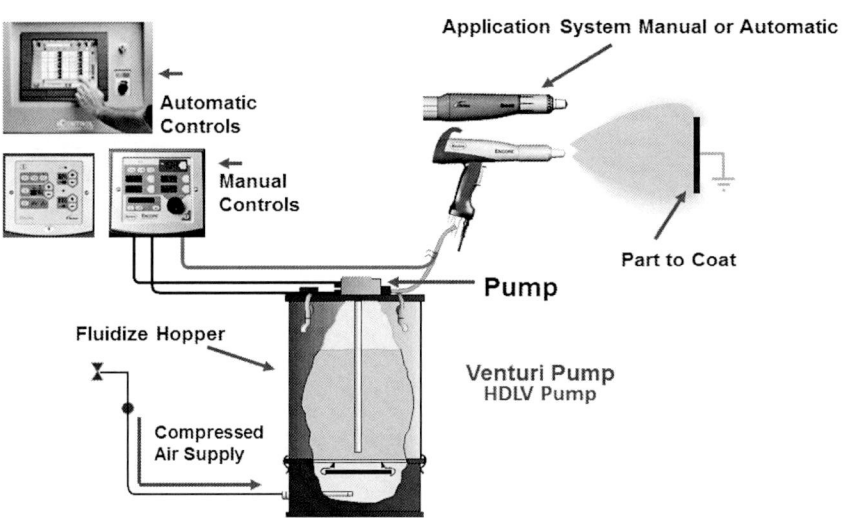

Figure 1. Overview of the powder application process

Figure 2 illustrates the variables that can be controlled automatically with electronic controls like Nordson iControls. Reducing variability by utilizing automatic controls reduces rejects, parts wear, and material consumption.

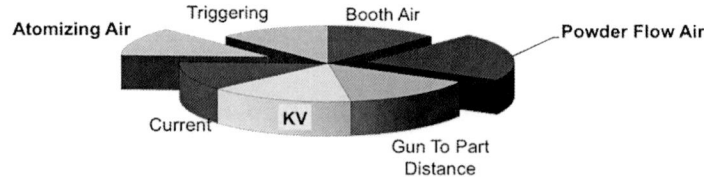

Figure 2. Powder application variables

Most of the focus on optimizing transfer efficiency has been on electrostatics and charging system controls. Factors affecting corona charging are:

- ✓ Field Strength
    - o Electrostatic parameters (kV: mA)
    - o Gun-to-part distance
    - o Electrode/nozzle configuration
- ✓ Particle Size
    - o Powder particles acquire a charge while traveling from the gun to the part through the electric field or corona discharge
- ✓ Charging Time
    - o Gun-to-part distance
    - o Powder velocity
    - o Electrode/nozzle configuration

A charged particle in an electric field is attracted to a part because of electrostatic charge, and that attraction is influenced by aerodynamic forces. Powder particles are easily influenced by competing airflow. The charge must be strong and velocity in spray area must be low for high transfer efficiency.

To optimize transfer efficiency, also optimize the aerodynamics of a powder application process by addressing:

- ✓ The spray pattern dynamics of an applicator
- ✓ Working characteristics of a powder pump

- ✓ Powder-to-air ratio
- ✓ Aerodynamic turbulence in the powder deposition area

The powder pump is designed to deliver powder to the applicator in a controlled, consistent, and uniform flow. This has been conventionally accomplished through the use of Venturi pumping. The powder pump is designed to deliver powder to the applicator in a controlled, consistent, and uniform flow. Powder flow air and atomizing air are balanced to provide a consistent flow of powder without surging or spitting. In addition the fluidizing pressure plays a major role in providing an even flow of powder to the gun.

The goal for a new Venturi powder pump is to improve performance by increasing powder output with less compressed air for higher performance and energy savings. The lower the velocity at the gun, the more powder on the part on the first pass. Additional design improvements are the powder hose and Venturi nozzles positively retained (versus o-ring fit) with quick-disconnect airline fittings. Figure 3 shows the increase in powder flow with new model Encore Venturi porcelain enamel powder pump compared to the old model 100 plus pump. Both used 12.7 mm inner diameter 12 m long delivery hose. The Encore pump delivered 20-30% more powder.

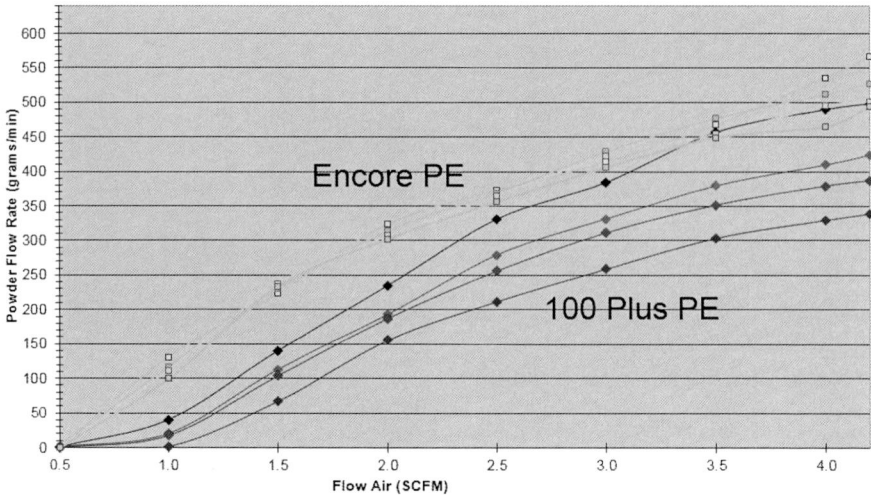

Figure 3. Porcelain enamel pump comparison

Using dense phase pumping the Prodigy HDLV pumps use less compressed air to propel powder to the gun for less air velocity, less overspray, and more powder on the part. At the center of dense phase technology is the HDLV (High Density Low Velocity) pump shown in Figure 4. It resembles a human heart in that it consists of two side by side pumps each with an upper and lower chamber working together to provide precise, carefully synchronized powder transport. With dense phase pump technology, the spray pattern is formed independently of powder transport so minimal air volume is required for powder delivery. The dense phase pump works without moving parts, is designed to purge and color change quickly, has a see-through design for easy diagnostics, and has up to 27 kg/hr (59 lbs/hr) output.

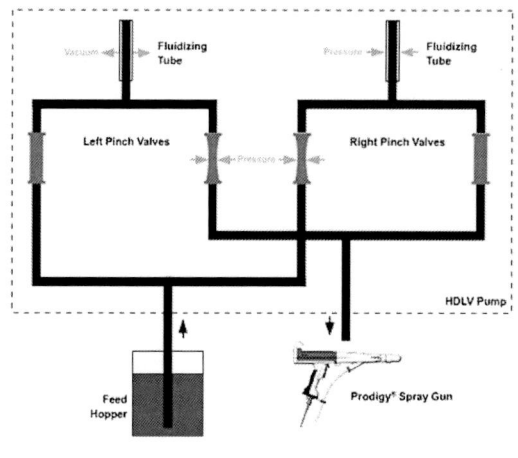 

(a) (b)

Figure 4. Dense phase pump technology (a) schematic and (b) appearance

Table 1 compares the powder hose inner diameters, flow rates, and gun-to-part distance with the two pumping technologies. The higher powder density of HDLV allows a narrower hose and requires a closer gun-to-part distance.

	Venturi	**HDLV**
Powder Hose ID (mm)	12.7	6.0
Powder Flow Rate (lbs/hr)	35	70
Gun-to-Part Distance (in)	6 to 10	3 to 6

Table 1. Comparison of venture and HDLV pumps

Optimal powder application combines the best technologies for powder application, as shown in Figure 5. The increased uniform flow of Encore is suitable for the oven doors, while the Prodigy HDLV provides pinpoint re-enforcement of the oven cavity in (b).

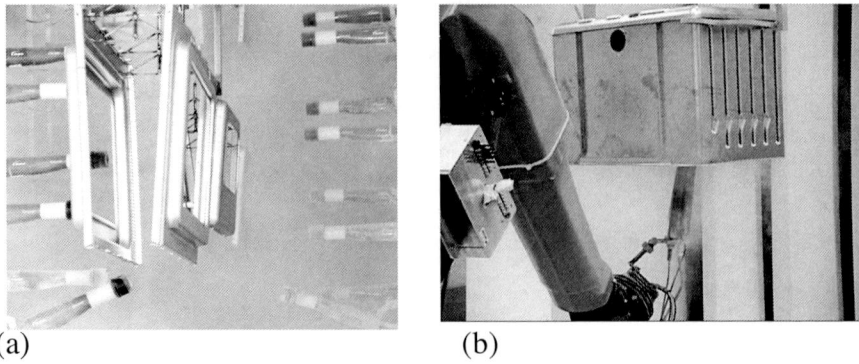

Figure 5. New installations with (a) Encore with venture pumps and (b) Prodigy with HDLV pumps

Powder Porcelain Rooms, Blow-Off and Hanger Cleaners

Mike Horton
KMI Systems Inc.

The recent installation of a new powder environmental room created a clean space with temperature and water vapor control for powder porcelain application, powder storage, and air flow control around powder booths.

The room walls were 24 gauge pre-painted skin on both sides with a 20 year paint guaranteed from manufacturer, laminated to 3" – 2 lb. foamed polyurethane with a "R" rating of 13. Clear anodized aluminum extrusions were used for the floor channel, "H" beams, proprietary 2-piece for the electrical chase, etc. Structural steel tubing of 6" x 3" was used as the vertical support structure for the room. Spanning the entire width of the room, this tubing supports the structural bar joists in addition to the ceiling panels, roof decking, lights, and the conveyor system.

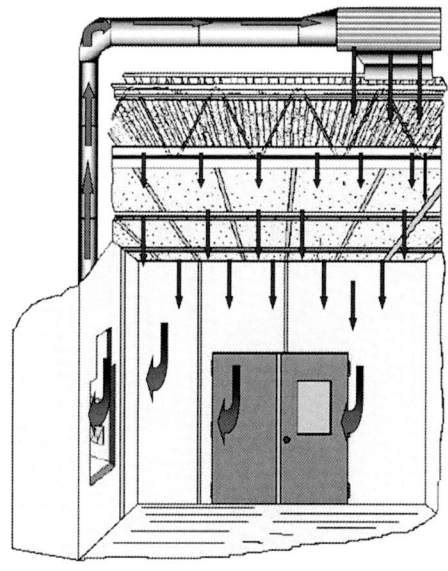

Figure 1. Air flow into room

As shown in Figure 1, conditioned air is introduced into the plenum ceiling, then spreads through the entire room. The bar joist slots form a slot diffuser system and distribute the air, creating a virtually perfect laminar "soft" flow throughout the room. The air is then drawn into the entrance and exit conveyor vestibules for recirculation back to the air conditioning system, creating a "closed loop" system. Exposed surfaces that could collect dust were avoided.

The personnel access doors were UL-Labeled 3'-0" x 7'-0" painted steel doors with half glass (24" x 30" safety glass), door closure, and passage hardware (keyed available). The roll-up doors were insulated with 2 lb. polyurethane insulation with manual chain pull operation (with motorized available as an option). Lighting was 400 Watt metal halide fixtures with anodized aluminum reflectors enclosed with clear tempered glass lenses. Lighting was installed flush with the ceiling panels to avoid collecting dust.

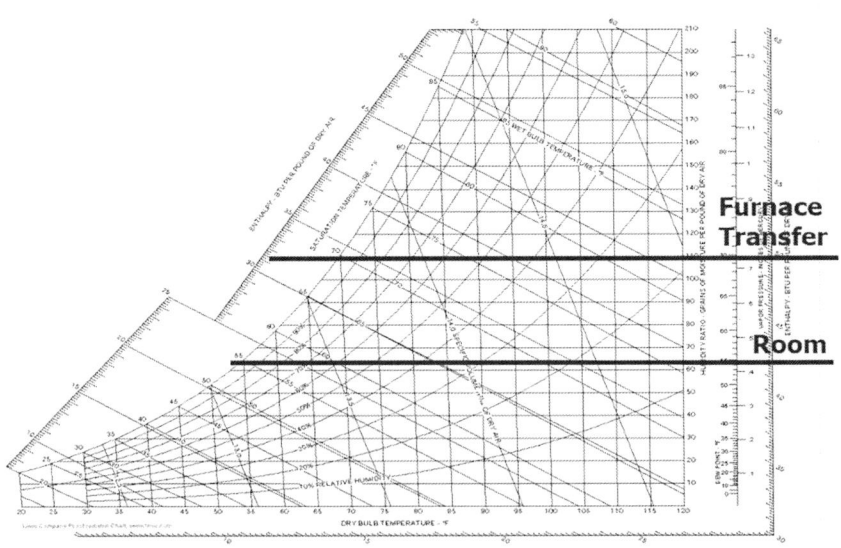

Figure 2. Room environmental operation parameters

Temperature and grains of water limits for the powder room are shown in Figure 2. The environmental control system was custom designed. All units used were UL Listed, CSA certified, and equipped with low ambient cooling option to 0°F (-18°C). The system heater section has electric, gas, steam, or hot water re-heat options. A correctly-sized heater section provides reheat to the system and energy for the de-humidification function.

The steam humidification system adds humidity to the room during dry conditions (e.g., winter in the US) to facilitate powder film build while avoid condensation. The system included microprocessor-based controls, digital display of operation, diagnostic capability, and proportional and integral controls (modulating not on/off) with control from the master control panel. The Direct Digital Control (DDC) environmental control system is able to monitor the environmental room via computer to run maintenance checks and help regulate the temperature and humidity control. Metasys Software Algorithms are used to coordinate humidification, de-humidification, air flow, cooling, and heating functions.

The environmental room shown in Figure 3 is a self-contained island to meet the requirements of the powder coating process. The "tri-flow" recovery vestibule system keeps cold air in the room and hot dirty air out. The filtering system contains two inch pleated pre-filter in conjunction with a four (4) stage extended surface cube filter as a final filter. This removes 100% of particles 2 microns or larger.

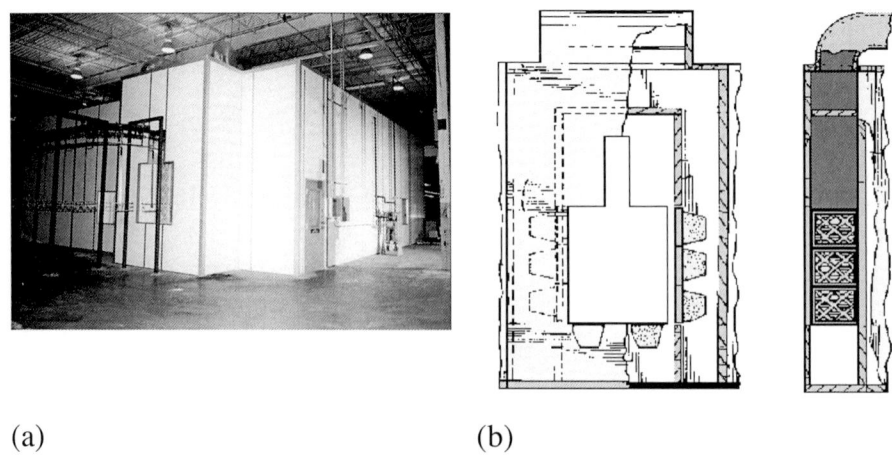

(a)   (b)

Figure 3. Vestibule (a) exterior and (b) cross-section

Controlling the environment in the part transfer room lowers moisture levels for furnace transfer to improve powder adhesion. It also supplies cooling air to personnel, reduces dust levels for operators, provides adequate lighting, and allows a process to blow-off defective parts and transport for re-coating (Figure 4). Dust collection and vacuum systems were included to keep dust off the floor.

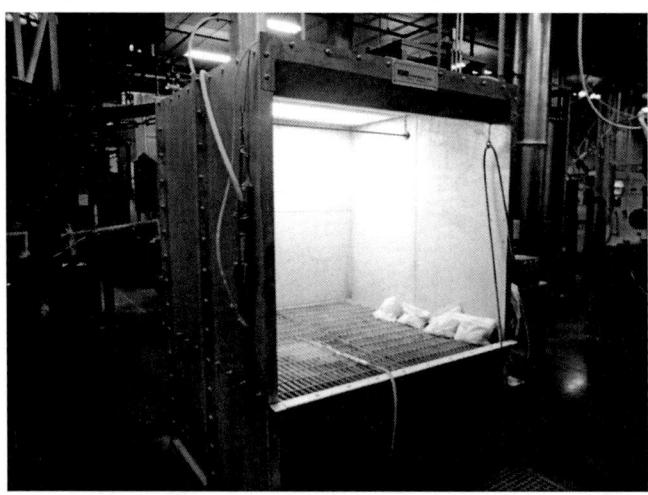

Figure 4. Part blow off booth

The objective for the hanger cleaner (Figure 5) is to remove powder frit coating from hangers, collect all particles to keep a clean environment, and reclaim all coating back to the powder booth. It is important to make sure the dust collector has sufficient capacity to keep up with the hanger cleaner. The reclaimed powder is screened (and could also be passed over magnets) before going back into the booth.

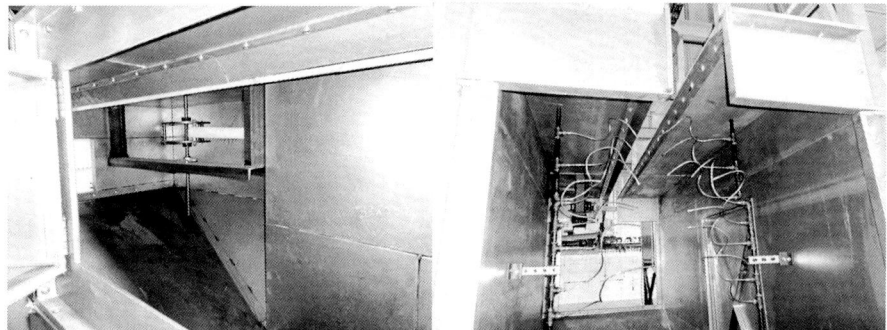

Figure 5. Hanger cleaning system

In summary, the newly constructed powder environmental room offered a suitable design for enamel application, climate control, and air flow control. Extension into the parts transfer area extends those controls.

Lean Six Sigma Overview

Walt Skovron
General Electric

What Lean Six Sigma is, why to use it, when to use it, and how to apply it to projects is discussed.

The implementation and components of Lean Six Sigma at General Electric (GE) are shown in Figure 1. Lean Six Sigma is used because good organizations need to respond to a constantly changing world with a clear strategy, engaged leadership, a motivated workforce, and effective management tools. Lean Six Sigma is the strategy for change. Customers are demanding more, competitors are doing more, employees want to do more, and global market pace is faster. The business world is changing as never before, and lean six sigma is a disciplined response to change.

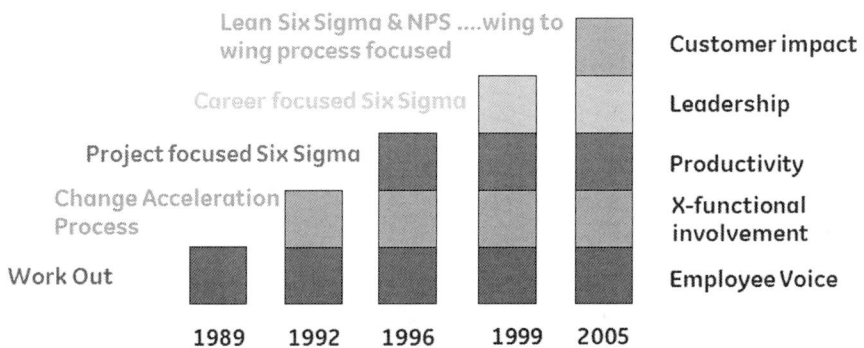

Figure 1. Evolution of six sigma at General Electric

Lean Six Sigma creates capacity to fund growth by freeing people from non-value added work. It stimulates increased revenues by improving cycle times, being faster to the market with less defects. It is a strategy, a discipline, leadership development, and common language that can make you "better and faster" everywhere. Lean

Six Sigma applies to every function:

- Human Resources - Staffing, Healthcare Costs
- Engineering - Design For Reliability, Drawing Accuracy
- Finance - Billing Timeliness and Accuracy, Risk Analysis
- Legal - Contract and Document Standardization, Compliance
- Manufacturing - Defect Reduction, Cycle-time Improvements
- Services - Accurate appointment times, Repair Turnaround
- Sourcing - Vendor Selection, Deflation
- Info. Technology - Application Development, System Efficiency
- Distribution - On-time transportation, Inventory control
- Sales - Face time, Accurate Orders, Timely Quotations

If there is an output, there is a process and Lean Six Sigma will work. Lean attacks waste by reducing non value added time spent on work. Six sigma attacks and minimizes variation. There is a focus on continuous improvement. For example, in a manufacturing process, lean reduces cycle times and eliminates waste. Six sigma reduces defects.

Everyone is involved in Lean Six Sigma:

- Champions: Fully-trained business leaders who own the processes and lead the deployment of Lean Six Sigma in a significant area of the business
- Master Black Belts: Fully-trained, full-time cross-functional quality leaders who team with champions and are jointly responsible for Lean Six Sigma strategy, training, mentoring, deployment and results
- Black Belts: Fully-trained, full-time Lean Six Sigma experts who lead improvement teams, work projects across functions in all areas of the business and mentor Green Belts
- Green Belts: Fully-trained individuals who use Lean Six Sigma skills to complete projects in their job areas
- Team Members: Individuals who receive specific Lean Six Sigma training and who support projects in their areas

Lean is the relentless pursuit of the perfect process through waste elimination:

"All we are doing is looking at a time line from the moment the customer gives us an order to the point when we collect the cash. And we are reducing that time line by removing the non-value added wastes"

>Taiichi Ohno
>Founder, Toyota Production System (TPS)

For Six Sigma, there are two meanings of "Sigma". The term "sigma" is used to designate the distribution or spread about the mean (average) of any process or procedure. For a business or manufacturing process, the sigma capability (z-value) is a metric that indicates how well that process is performing. The higher the sigma capability, the better. Sigma capability measures the capability of the process to perform defect-free work. A defect is anything that results in customer dissatisfaction. As defects go down, the Sigma Capability goes up.

Lean Six Sigma is a powerful way to improve processes because it is:

- Focused on customer value
- A way to solve problems to enable you to do your job effectively
- A method to make data-driven decisions
- Focused on reducing process inefficiency and cycle time and improving quality
- Disciplined approach to identify opportunities to improve and design products and processes
- Common language across GE
- Both philosophy and methodology

It is NOT:

- An end in itself
- A replacement for engineering, scientific or process knowledge
- Just a set of tools
- Applicable to every problem in its entirety

Sigma capability of two is 99% good but still means 308,537 defects per million. An increase to six means only 3.4. The level of defect reduction in real life examples possible when the sigma capability is increased from the classical view of quality of 99% good and Z = 3.8 to 99.99966% good and the six sigma level are striking:

The Classical View of Quality
"99% Good" (Z = 3.8s)
- 20,000 lost articles of mail per hour
- Unsafe drinking water almost 15 minutes each day
- 5,000 incorrect surgical operations per week
- 2 short or long landings at most major airports daily
- 200,000 wrong drug prescriptions each year
- No electricity for almost 7 hours each month

The Six Sigma View of Quality
"99.99966% Good" (Z = 6s)
- Seven lost articles of mail per hour
- One minute of unsafe drinking water every seven months
- 1.7 incorrect surgical operations per week
- One short or long landing at most major airports every five years
- 68 wrong drug prescriptions each year
- One hour without electricity every 34 years

For problem solving, if we understand that "X" is the cause, why do we constantly test and inspect Y? Lean Six Sigma provides statistical solutions to problems. High level process maps are made to determine when a problem is occurring using the six sigma tool set and the process of Define, Measure, Analyze, Improve, and Control (DMAIC):

1. Define
    a. What is important to customer [critical to quality (CTQs)]?
    b. Define the "Y"
2. Measure
    a. How is the process (The Y) performing for the customers (capability)?
    b. How good could the process be (entitlement)?
    c. How good is the data? Can I rely on it (gage R&R)?
    d. Measure the "Y"
3. Analyze
    a. What are the critical defects causing variation?
    b. What % of variation?
    c. Find & Measure the "Xs"
4. Improve
    a. How do we fix the critical defects (Xs)?
    b. What % of variation in critical Xs can I remove?
    c. Improve the "Xs"
5. Control
    a. How can we maintain the improvements?
    b. Control the "Xs" So Customer Never Sees Variation in the "Y"
    c. $Y = f(x_1, x_2, x_3 ...)$

If you know what you need to do, just go do it. If your car has a flat tire, fix it. If you do not know what to do (your car will not start), data and analysis are needed to fix the problem and apply Lean Six Sigma.

Innovative Metallic Effect Frit for Oven Cavity - Pyrolytic KIRA

Hidekazu Onishi[1], Hiroshi Iwamura[1], Shinichi Kuwae[2],
Michael E. Tracey[3]
[1]*Tokan Material Technology Co., Ltd.*
[2]*TOMATEC FINE MATERIALS CO., LTD.*
[3]*TOMATEC (AMERICA), Inc.*

To keep the interior of oven cavities clean, the liner enamels have a self-cleaning function. The typical kinds of self-cleaning systems are catalytic and pyrolytic. The catalytic self-cleaning makes use of the ability of metallic oxides bonded to the enamel to decompose food stains at food cooking temperatures. However, the catalytic self-cleaning enamel has a rough surface, which is easily stained with oil and food. Additionally, the only way of decorating of the surface is by stippling, which is an extra process. On the other hand, pyrolytic enamel is tougher, it has a smooth surface, and it can have several types of appearance. Pyrolytic oven cavity generally is dark color, such as dark blue and black, and often with white mottle formulated into the enamel. A new type of appearance has been developed called "KIRA", which is enamel with a metallic effect on its surface to provide a new appearance to pyrolytic self-cleaning enamels.

Introduction

"KIRA" is enamel with a metallic effect. In most cases, metallic pigments added to conventional enamel have a tendency to be dissolved during firing because of the alkali contents in the enamel. An enamel has been developed that does not dissolve metallic pigments.

In the photos shown in Figure 1, as firing temperature was increased, the particle size of metallic pigments added to a conventional enamel decreased. The metallic pigments were dissolved during firing. In this case, the metallic effect is not visible on the enamel surface. In the case of "KIRA", bigger particles as visible in Figure 2, even at higher temperatures. The metallic pigments hardly dissolve into enamel solution, and the metallic effect is readily visible.

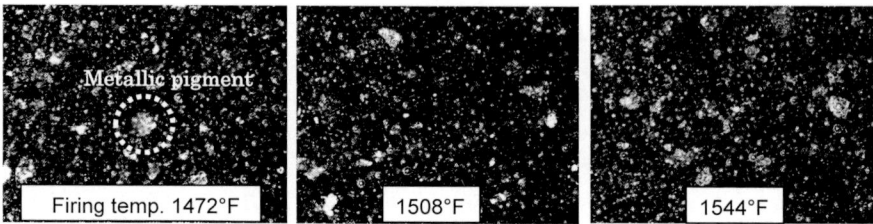

Figure 1. Micrograph of conventional enamel surface

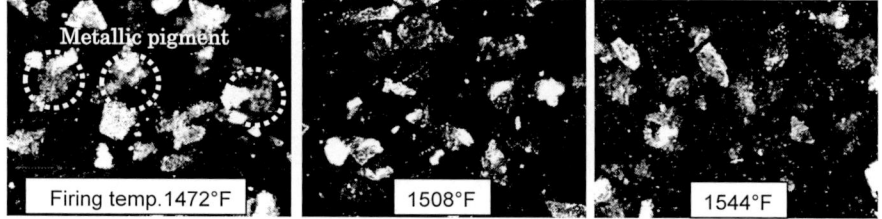

Figure 2. Micrograph of "KIRA" enamel surface

Improving the Pyrolytic Enamel

The goals of the coating properties were:

- Appearance: smooth, glossy, metallic effect.
- Acid resistance: AA (citric acid at room temperature).
- Heat resistance: after heating at 990°F, 48 hours, the appearance is unchanged.

Various frits, additives, pigments and so on were tested to determine the formulation of the new enamel.

Result

The most important characteristic for the fired enamel to have both pyrolytic self-clean ability and the metallic effect. First, the improved enamel has excellent metallic effect compared to a conventional acid-resistant enamel. A new frit composition was used to prevent dissolution of the metallic pigments into the enamel. Second, both the conventional and improved enamel had AA spot acid resistance. The heat resistance test, which is one of the characteristics of pyrolytic self-cleaning, was carried out under the conditions of 990°F for 48 hours. After heating, the gloss of the improved enamel was compared to the conventional enamel. The gloss of conventional enamel surface was reduced and showed a lot of edge metallization. On the other hand, the gloss of the improved enamel surface changed less after the test. However, the improved enamel showed weak adherence on cleaned only steel. This was improved by application to nickel flashed steel. Additionally, thermal shock resistance testing was carried out by putting a specimen into a furnace at an elevated temperature for 20 minutes then dropping into 77°F water. At about 160 μm (5 mils) of thickness, conventional enamel cracked when it dropped from 750°F to 77°F. In contrast, the improved enamel did not crack under the same conditions.

Conclusion

A metallic effect was added to pyrolytic enamel. Improved enamel (Pyrolytic KIRA) has better heat resistance and metallic effect than conventional enamel.

Migration Testing of Enamels for Direct Contact with Drinking Water

Eckhard Voss
Wendel Email

Porcelain enamel (also called vitreous enamel) has been used for a very long time as a durable coating in food contact on cookware and in contact with drinking water in water heaters, valves, tanks, pipes etc. A migration study was conducted to analyse the leaching of metals of concern versus current allowable limits.

Introduction

Porcelain enamel has excellent resistance to chemical attack by food, acids and water at low and high temperatures. As such, porcelain enamel is highly suitable for use as a protective coating in contact with water meant for human consumption for many products such as water heaters, tanks, storage systems, pipes, valves, and joints.

European drinking water regulations are being modified to specify limits for low level contaminants in both cold and hot water. For example, in Germany, the UBA (Umweltbundesamt = Federal Environmental Office) requires all appliances to meet German specifications for water quality regardless of where the appliance was produced. Germany, France, the Netherlands, and the United Kingdom have agreed to cooperate to harmonize the testing of the hygienic suitability of products which come into contact with drinking water.

A migration study with ten enamelled water heaters was carried out (as reported by EG-CPDW 238 rev.2 on October 31, 2006) to validate the Positive Vitreous Enamels Oxide Composition List (OCL) proposed by the International Enamelling Institute (IEI) with the goal of obtaining an Accepted Without Testing (AWT) procedure for Acceptance of Vitreous/Porcelain Enamel in the framework of the Construction Products in contact with Drinking Water (CPDW) Directive. This migration study, carried out by wet chemical analysis using inductively coupled plasma mass spectroscopy (ICP/MS), aimed to prove that porcelain enamels readily meet the Drinking Water Parameters of the Drinking Water Directive (DWD) 98/83 CE.

EG-PDWD requested European porcelain enamelers for a second migration study, to be carried out with ICP/MS analysis to test for metals such as nickel (Ni), lead (Pb), cadmium (Cd), and antimony (Sb). The ICP/MS analysis of the second migration study were run at TWZ-D. A literature review of general scientific/technical information about enameling was conducted as part of the second migration study.[1,2,3,11,12,13].

Procedures

Three grades of coatings were selected from the ten samples of the first migration study to be subjected to the 85°C (185°F) hot water attack for extraction testing of the aforementioned metals. These glasses are characterized by the hot stage microscope (HSM) curves shown in Figure 1.

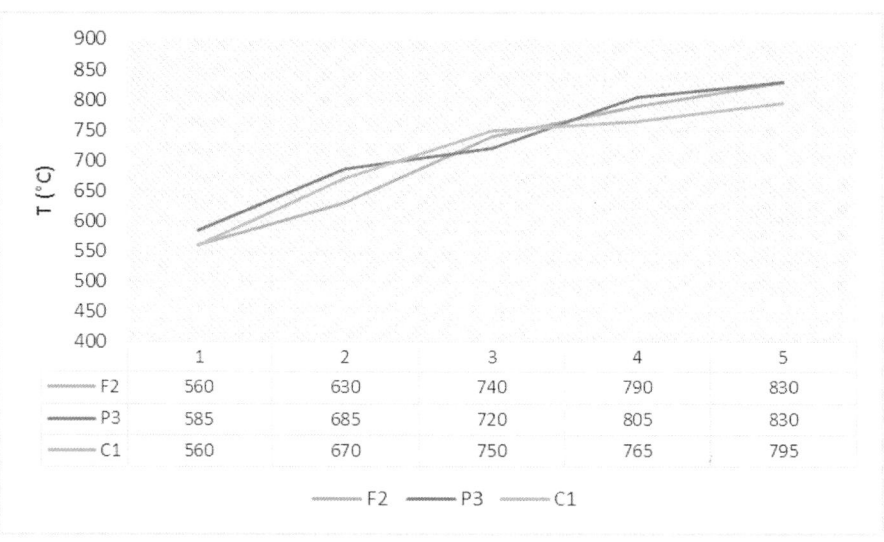

Figure 1. Hot stage microscope fingerprint of tested enamels

The oxide composition of these three enamels are within the Oxide

Composition List (OCL) proposed as an approved list of porcelain enamels shown in Table 1 that have very high hot water resistance per standard DIN 4753-3 "Porcelain Enamel on Boilers and Water Heaters:

Substance	Min	Max	Substance	Min	Max	Substance	Min	Max
SiO_2	40	80	MgO	0	2	Fe_2O_3	0	5
B_2O_3	5	15	CeO_2	0	15	MoO_3	0	3
Na_2O	5	20	ZnO	0	10	P_2O_5	0	5
K_2O	0	5	Al_2O_3	0	5	SnO_2	0	5
Li_2O	0	10	CoO	0	3	TiO_2	0	10
CaO	0	10	NiO	0	3	ZrO_2	0	20
BaO	0	5	CuO	0	2	F	0	5
SrO	0	5	MnO_2	0	3			

Requirements and Tests" published in February 2013.

Table 1. Vitreous enamel positive Oxide Composition List (OCL)

The migration study parameters are summarized in Table 2. Water resistance was measured using DIN4753-3 "Porcelain Enamel on Boilers and Water Heaters: Requirements and Tests" with test water with a conductivity of 1 µS/m, 2 cycles of 504 hours, 100°C (212°F) water, and the water changed every 24 hours during the workweek and every 48 hours during the weekend. Samples were prepared according to EN12873-1 "Influence of Materials on Water Intended for Human Consumption – Influence Due to Migration – Part 1: Test Method for Non-Metallic and Non-Cementitious Factory Made Products". The migration test used water distilled at Ferro with a pH of 5.9 and a conductivity of 0 µS/m at 22.1°C (71.8°F) as a worst case scenario because it is well established that the distilled water is much more aggressive than tap water because of the complete absence of solute.[11,12]

Enamel	DIN4753/3 Weight Loss (g/m2)	Water Quality	Sample Pretreatment	Migration Test Temperature (°C)	Migration Execution Testing Procedure	S/V dm^{-1}
F2	1.2	Distilled	EN12873-1	85	First 3+10°+11° Cycles 24h	5.3
P3	2.8	Distilled	EN12873-1	85	First 3+10°+11° Cycles 24h	5
C1	1.7	Distilled	EN12873-1	85	First 3+10°+11° Cycles 24h	5

Table 2. Migration test study parameters

The test method used for the migration study was as described in standard EN 12873-1 with a surface to volume (S/V) ratio of the extraction cell is ≥ 5 dm^{-1}. The leachates obtained after hot water exposure were sampled according to the schedule shown in Table 3.

Number migration periods/days	Days	Comment
1/1	Tuesday to Wednesday	24 h – analyzed
2/2	Wednesday to Thursday	24 h – analyzed
3/3	Thursday to Friday	24 h – analyzed
4/6	Friday to Monday	72 h
5/7	Monday to Tuesday	24 h
6/8	Tuesday to Wednesday	24 h
7/9	Wednesday to Thursday	24 h
8/10	Tuesday to Friday	24 h
9/13	Friday to Monday	72 h
10/14	Monday to Tuesday	24 h – analyzed [a]
11/15	Tuesday to Wednesday	24 h – analysed [a]

[a] If required

Table 3. Water sampling sequence from migration study

The migration testing carried out with the cell shown in Figure 2, derived from ISO 2734 with the geometrical characteristics specified by EN 12283-1.

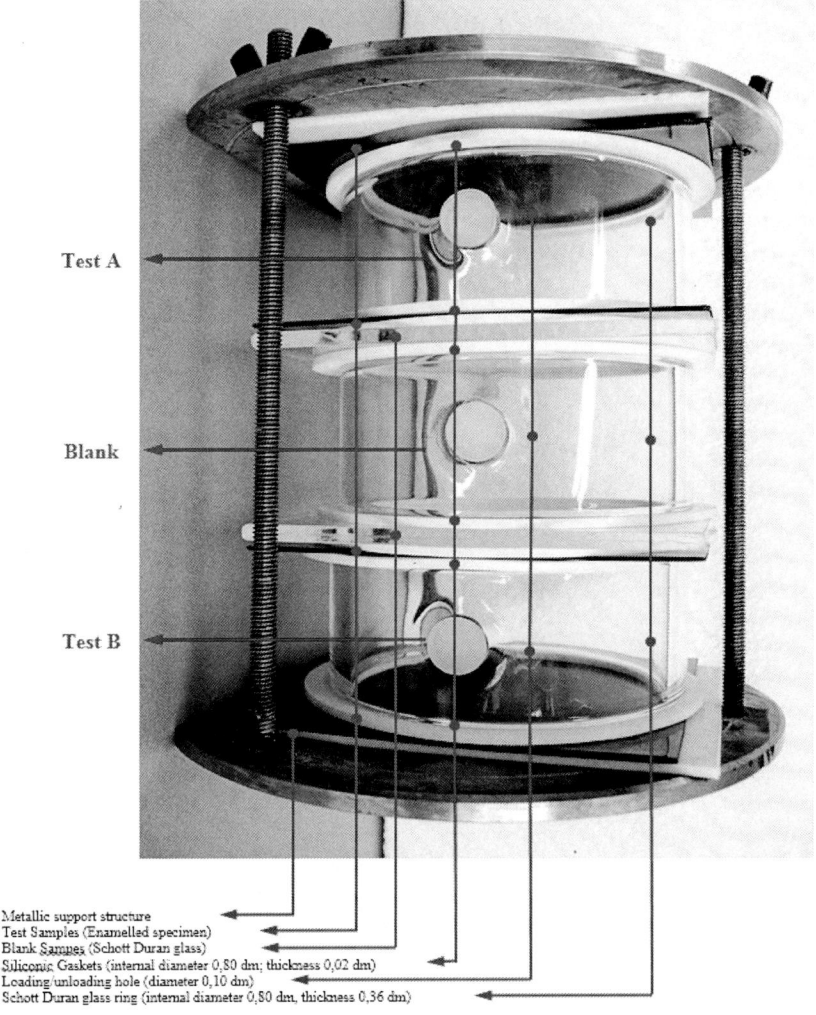

1) Metallic support structure
2) Test Samples (Enamelled specimen)
3) Blank Samples (Schott Duran glass)
4) Siliconic Gaskets (internal diameter 0,80 dm; thickness 0,02 dm)
5) Loading/unloading hole (diameter 0,10 dm)
6) Schott Duran glass ring (internal diameter 0,80 dm, thickness 0,36 dm)

Figure 2. Migration test apparatus

ICP/MS analysis method for detecting the amount of release of the elements in question was chosen to comply with the analytical accuracy requested by DWD 98/83/CE -Annex III and is shown in Table 4.

			E.D. 98/83/CE				
N°	Element	M.A.C.	Trueness % of Parametric Value	Precision % of Parametric Value	Lim. of Detection % of Parametric Value	% of Parametric Value	Analitical Method
		µg/l	µg/l	µg/l	µg/l	%	
1	B	1.000	100	100	100	10	ICP/MS
2	Ni	20	2	2	2	10	ICP/MS
3	Cu	2.000	200	200	200	10	ICP/MS
4	F	1.500	150	150	150	10	Ion Chromatography
5	Mn	50	5	5	5	10	ICP/MS
6	Pb	10	1	1	1	10	ICP/MS
7	Cd	5	0,5	0,5	0,5	10	ICP/MS
8	Sb	5	1,25	1,25	1,25	25	ICP/MS

Table 4. Accuracy of ICP/MS analysis

The real ICP/MS analytical accuracy of the analytical lab TWZ-D is reported in Table 5.

N°	Element	ED 98/83 CE M.A.C.	Trueness(') % of Parametric Value		Precision(') % of Parametric Value		Lim. of Determination(') % of Parametric Value	Analytical Method
		µg/L	%	µg/L	%	µg/L	µg/L	
1	B	1000	1,6	16	4,0	40,0	3,2	ICP/MS
2	Ni	20	0,7	0,14	2,0	0,4	0,3	ICP/MS
3	Cu	2000	1,3	26	2,5	50,0	1,2	ICP/MS
4	F	1500	5,1	76,5	3,5	52,5	15	Potentiometry
5	Mn	50	0,8	0,4	2,2	1,1	1,7	ICP/MS
6	Pb	10	0,8	0,08	2,0	0,2	0,2	ICP/MS
7	Cd	5	0,3	0,015	2,6	0,1	0,1	ICP/MS
8	Sb	5	0,3	0,015	1,9	0,1	0,3	ICP/MS

Table 5. Vitreous/porcelain enamel specifications for migration test analysis (source: TWZ-D)

Results

The results of the migration study are summarized in Tables 7, 8, and 9. Each table shows elements, the maximum allowed concentration (MAC) value (µg/l) of the DWD 98/83/CE, original oxide composition, and element concentrations in the 2 leachate samples versus a blank sample. Actual MAC values are subject to change as regulations are revised and vary from country to country. Furthermore, the average concentration of the elements of the two samples was calculated as well as the migration rate in 24 hours at 85°C (M^{85}_{24}) (µg * dm^{-2} * d) normalizing by S/V$_{test}$ rate and for 1 day (24 h) residence time.

To compare the migration results with the MAC value of DWD 98/83/CE, it was assumed $F_{go} = 1$. In this way the numerical value of M^{85}_{24} remains the same, but its measurement unit was comparable with MAC in µg/L or p.p.b. Based on prior knowledge in the enamelling industry as well as the conversion factors resulting from the EG-CPDW literature[14,15], this assumption is realistic. On the European market, the average Hot Water Tank S/V rate is very close to 1 dm^{-2} as shown in Table 9.

Capacity [dm^3]	Surface [dm^2]	S/V ratio [dm^{-1}]	European Average Turnover (%)	Average S/V ratio (ECC) [dm^{-1}]
10	33	3.3	3.10	0.10
15	34	2.26	4.70	0.11
30	54	1.8	4.10	0.07
50	70	1.4	8.20	0.11
80	100	1.25	20.70	0.26
100	117	1.17	21.70	0.25
120	124	1.03	6.90	0.07
150*	161	1.07	8.00	0.09
200*	203	1.01	12.50	0.13
300	277	0.9	10.10	0.09
		Total:	100.00	1.28

Table 9. Most common dimensions of European hot water tanks and boilers

From the Correction Factors equations :

- $C_{tap85°C}$ < M.A.C.(µg/l or µg/dm^3 or ppb)
- $M^{24}_{85°C}$ (µg/dm^2/day) = $C^{24}_{85°C}$ /(S/V)$_{test}$ = (µg/dm^3/day)/ dm^{-1}
- Fg = Geometrical Factor = S/V$_{product}$ (dm^{-1})
- Fo = Contact (Residence) Time = (day)
- Fgo = Fg x Fo (dm^{-1} x day)
- Ctap85°C = M24/85°C (185°F) x Fgo (µg/dm^3 or µg/l or ppb)

The Fgo Interval for the hot water tanks can be estimated given the following options[14,15]:

N°	Fg	×	Fo (day)	=	Fgo (dm^{-1} × day)
1	1	×	1	=	1
2	1	×	1/6	=	1/6
3	1	×	1/3	=	1/3
4	1	×	1/3	=	1/3
5	3.3	×	1/3	=	1.1 worse case

(Fg in dm^{-1})

To calculate Ctap85°C, option 1 from the Fgo interval was selected as the most realistic to be used as conversion factor because of the relatively long residence time used of 1 day as well as the real S/V ratio of actual water heaters. Another consideration is that no one drinks hot water at 85°C (185°F) although water at that temperature is used for cooking.

Migration Testing of Enamels for Direct Contact with Drinking Water

Ferro Electrostatic Powder F2 Standard EN 12873-1:2002 85 ± 2°C distilled water S/V = 5.25 dm^{-1} t(0) = 1

Element	MAC (μg/L)	Formula	%	OCL (%)	Test Water (mg/L)	Sample	Cycle 1 Migration (mg/L)	Cycle 1 Blank Test (mg/L)	Cycle 1 Migration Rate (μg/dm²/day)	Cycle 2 Migration (mg/L)	Cycle 2 Blank Test (mg/L)	Cycle 2 Migration Rate (μg/dm²/day)	Cycle 3 Migration (mg/L)	Cycle 3 Blank Test (mg/L)	Cycle 3 Migration Rate (μg/dm²/day)	Cycle 4 Migration (mg/L)	Cycle 4 Blank Test (mg/L)	Cycle 4 Migration Rate (μg/dm²/day)	Cycle 5 Migration (mg/L)	Cycle 5 Blank Test (mg/L)	Cycle 5 Migration Rate (μg/dm²/day)
B	1000	B_2O_3	10.4	5 - 15	<20	1	270	40	43.0	260	30	43.0	390	20	69.2	1140	50	203.7	1390	20	256.1
						2	440		74.8	740		132.7	1080		198.1	800		140.2	1380		254.2
						Average			58.9			87.9			133.7			172.0			255.2
Ni	20	NiO	0.98	0 - 3	<1	1	34	2	6.0	18	1	3.2	11	2	1.7	<1	2	-0.2	1	1	0.0
						2	9		1.3	4		0.6	2		0.0	<1		-0.2	<1		0.0
						Average			3.7			1.9			0.9			-0.2			0.0
Cu	2000	CuO	0.94	0 - 2	<10	1	20	<10	3.7	<10	<10	1.9	<10	<10	1.9	<10	<10	1.9	<10	<10	1.9
						2	<10		1.9	<10		1.9	<10		1.9	<10		1.9	<10		1.9
						Average			2.8			1.9			1.9			1.9			1.9
Mn	50	MnO_2	1.19	0 - 3	<5	1	49	6	8.0	31	<5	5.8	15	<5	2.8	<5	<5	0.9	<5	<5	0.9
						2	8		0.3	<5		0.9	<5		0.9	<5		0.9	<5		0.9
						Average			4.2			3.4			1.9			0.9			0.9
F	1500	F	0.75	0 - 5	<50	1	<50	<50	9.3	<50	<50	9.3	<50	<50	9.3	<50	<50	9.3	<50	<50	9.3
						2	<50		9.3	<50		9.3	<50		9.3	<50		9.3	<50		9.3
						Average			9.3			9.3			9.3			9.3			9.3
Sb	5	Sb_2O_3	<Lim	-	<1	1	2	<1	0.4	1	<1	0.2	2	<1	0.4	5	<1	0.9	6	<1	1.1
						2	2		0.4	3		0.6	5		0.9	3		0.6	4		0.7
						Average			0.4			0.4			0.7			0.8			0.9
Pb	10	PbO	<Lim	-	<1	1	<1	<1	0.2	<1	<1	0.2	<1	<1	0.2	<1	<1	0.2	<1	<1	0.2
						2	<1		0.2	<1		0.2	<1		0.2	<1		0.2	<1		0.2
						Average			0.2			0.2			0.2			0.2			0.2
Cd	5	CdO	<Lim	-	<0.1	1	<0.1	0.2	-0.02	<0.1	<0.1	0.02	<0.1	0.1	0.02	<0.1	<0.1	0.02	<0.1	<0.1	0.02
						2	<0.1		-0.02	<0.1		0.02	<0.1		0.02	<0.1		0.02	<0.1		0.02
						Average			-0.02			0.02			0.02			0.02			0.02

Table 6. Migration test data for enamel F2

Migration Testing of Enamels for Direct Contact with Drinking Water

Pemco Electrostatic Powder P3 Standard EN 12873-1:2002 85 ± 2°C distilled water S/V = 5 dm^{-1} t(0) = 1

Element	MAC (µg/L)	Formula	%	OCl (%)	Test Water (mg/L)	Sample	Cycle 1 Migration (mg/L)	Cycle 1 Blank Test (mg/L)	Cycle 1 Migration Rate (µg/dm²/day)	Cycle 2 Migration (mg/L)	Cycle 2 Blank Test (mg/L)	Cycle 2 Migration Rate (µg/dm²/day)	Cycle 3 Migration (mg/L)	Cycle 3 Blank Test (mg/L)	Cycle 3 Migration Rate (µg/dm²/day)	Cycle 4 Migration (mg/L)	Cycle 4 Blank Test (mg/L)	Cycle 4 Migration Rate (µg/dm²/day)	Cycle 5 Migration (mg/L)	Cycle 5 Blank Test (mg/L)	Cycle 5 Migration Rate (µg/dm²/day)
B	1000	B_2O_3	11.3	5 - 15	< 20	1	420	30	78.0	1570	30	308.0	1910	40	374.0	1630	20	322.0	1880	40	368.0
						2	820		158.0	1760		346.0	1920		376.0	1660		328.0	1850		364.0
						Average			*118.0*			*327.0*			*375.0*			*325.0*			*366.0*
Ni	20	NiO	0.98	0 - 3	< 1	1	19	1	3.6	4	< 1	0.8	4	3	0.2	2	2	0.0	2	1	0.2
						2	6		1.0	3		0.6	4		0.2	2		0.0	3		0.4
						Average			*2.3*			*0.7*			*0.2*			*0.0*			*0.3*
Cu	2000	CuO	0.94	0 - 2	< 10	1	< 10	10	0.0	< 10	< 10	2.0	< 10	< 10	2.0	< 10	< 10	2.0	< 10	< 10	2.0
						2	< 10		0.0	< 10		2.0	< 10		2.0	< 10		2.0	< 10		2.0
						Average			*0.0*			*2.0*			*2.0*			*2.0*			*2.0*
Mn	50	MnO_2	1.19	0 - 3	< 5	1	13	< 5	2.6	< 5	< 5	1.0	< 5	< 5	1.0	< 5	< 5	1.0	< 5	< 5	1.0
						2	< 5		1.0	< 5		1.0	< 5		1.0	< 5		1.0	< 5		1.0
						Average			*1.8*			*1.0*			*1.0*			*1.0*			*1.0*
F	1500	F	0.75	0 - 5	< 50	1	< 50	< 50	10.0	< 50	< 50	10.0	< 50	< 50	10.0	< 50	< 50	10.0	< 50	< 50	10.0
						2	< 50		10.0	< 50		10.0	< 50		10.0	< 50		10.0	< 50		10.0
						Average			*10.0*			*10.0*			*10.0*			*10.0*			*10.0*
Sb	5	Sb_2O_3	<Lim	-	< 1	1	< 1	< 1	0.2	< 1	< 1	0.2	< 1	< 1	0.2	< 1	< 1	0.2	< 1	< 1	0.2
						2	< 1		0.2	< 1		0.2	< 1		0.2	< 1		0.2	< 1		0.2
						Average			*0.2*			*0.2*			*0.2*			*0.2*			*0.2*
Pb	10	PbO	<Lim	-	< 1	1	< 1	< 1	0.2	< 1	< 1	0.2	< 1	< 1	0.2	< 1	< 1	0.2	< 1	< 1	0.2
						2	< 1		0.2	< 1		0.2	< 1		0.2	< 1		0.2	< 1		0.2
						Average			*0.2*			*0.2*			*0.2*			*0.2*			*0.2*
Cd	5	CdO	<Lim	-	< 0.1	1	< 0.1	< 0.1	0.02	< 0.1	< 0.1	0.02	< 0.1	0.1	0.02	< 0.1	< 0.1	0.02	< 0.1	< 0.1	0.02
						2	< 0.1		0.02	< 0.1		0.02	< 0.1		0.02	< 0.1		0.02	< 0.1		0.02
						Average			*0.02*			*0.02*			*0.02*			*0.02*			*0.02*

Table 7. Migration test data for enamel P3

Element	Formula	MAC (µg/L)	%	OCL [%]	Test Water (mg/L)	Sample	Cycle 1 Migration (mg/L)	Cycle 1 Blank Test (mg/L)	Cycle 1 Migration Rate (µg/dm²/day)	Cycle 2 Migration (mg/L)	Cycle 2 Blank Test (mg/L)	Cycle 2 Migration Rate (µg/dm²/day)	Cycle 3 Migration (mg/L)	Cycle 3 Blank Test (mg/L)	Cycle 3 Migration Rate (µg/dm²/day)	Cycle 4 Migration (mg/L)	Cycle 4 Blank Test (mg/L)	Cycle 4 Migration Rate (µg/dm²/day)	Cycle 5 Migration (mg/L)	Cycle 5 Blank Test (mg/L)	Cycle 5 Migration Rate (µg/dm²/day)
B	B_2O_3	1000	10	5 - 15	< 20	1	790	30	152.0	740	20	144.0	810	20	158.0	370	20	70.0	360	20	68.0
						2	800		154.0	720		140.0	760		148.0	390		74.0	360		68.0
						Average			*153.0*			*142.0*			*153.0*			*72.0*			*68.0*
Ni	NiO	20	0.5	0 - 3	< 1	1	1	<1	0.0	1	<1	0.2	1	<1	0.0	1	<1	0.0	1	<1	0.0
						2	1		0.0	1		0.2	1		0.0	1		0.0	1		0.0
						Average			*0.0*			*0.2*			*0.0*			*0.0*			*0.0*
Cu	CuO	2000	0.3	0 - 2	< 10	1	10	<10	2.0	10	<10	2.0	<10	<10	2.0	<10	<10	2.0	<10	<10	2.0
						2	10		2.0	10		2.0	10		2.0	<10		2.0	40		8.0
						Average			*2.0*			*2.0*			*2.0*			*2.0*			*5.0*
Mn	MnO_2	50	0.5	0 - 3	< 5	1	<5	<5	1.0	<5	<5	1.0	<5	<5	1.0	<5	<5	1.0	<5	<5	1.0
						2	<5		1.0	<5		1.0	<5		1.0	<5		1.0	<5		1.0
						Average			*1.0*			*1.0*			*1.0*			*1.0*			*1.0*
F	F	1500	1.7	0 - 5	< 50	1	<50	<50	10.0	<50	<50	10.0	<50	<50	10.0	<50	<50	10.0	<50	<50	10.0
						2	<50		10.0	<50		10.0	<50		10.0	<50		10.0	<50		10.0
						Average			*10.0*			*10.0*			*10.0*			*10.0*			*10.0*
Sb	Sb_2O_3	5	<Lim	-	< 1	1	<1	<1	0.2	<1	<1	0.2	<1	<1	0.2	<1	<1	0.2	<1	<1	0.2
						2	<1		0.2	<1		0.2	<1		0.2	<1		0.2	<1		0.2
						Average			*0.2*			*0.2*			*0.2*			*0.2*			*0.2*
Pb	PbO	10	<Lim	-	< 1	1	<1	<1	0.2	<1	<1	0.2	<1	<1	0.2	<1	<1	0.2	<1	<1	0.2
						2	<1		0.2	<1		0.2	<1		0.2	<1		0.2	<1		0.2
						Average			*0.2*			*0.2*			*0.2*			*0.2*			*0.2*
Cd	CdO	5	<Lim	-	< 0.1	1	<0.1	<0.1	0.02	<0.1	<0.1	0.02	<0.1	0.1	0.02	<0.1	<0.1	0.02	<0.1	<0.1	0.02
						2	<0.1		0.02	<0.1		0.02	<0.1		0.02	<0.1		0.02			0.02
						Average			*0.02*			*0.02*			*0.02*			*0.02*			*0.02*

Colorobbia Electrostatic Powder C1 Standard EN 12873-1:2002 85 ± 2°C distilled water S/V = 5 dm^{-1} t(0) = 1

Table 8. Migration test data for enamel C1

Figure 3 and Figure 4 show the levels of eight different elements after the migration test.

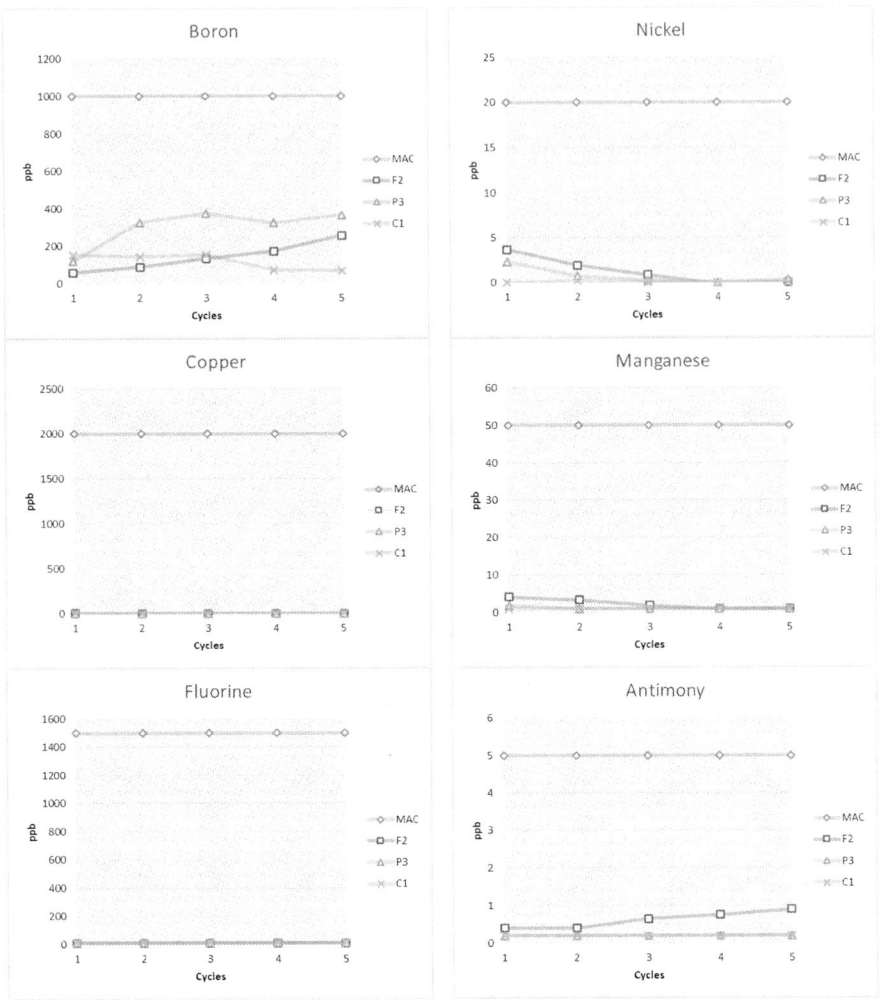

Figure 3. Migration tests for boron, nickel, copper, manganese, fluorine, and antimony levels

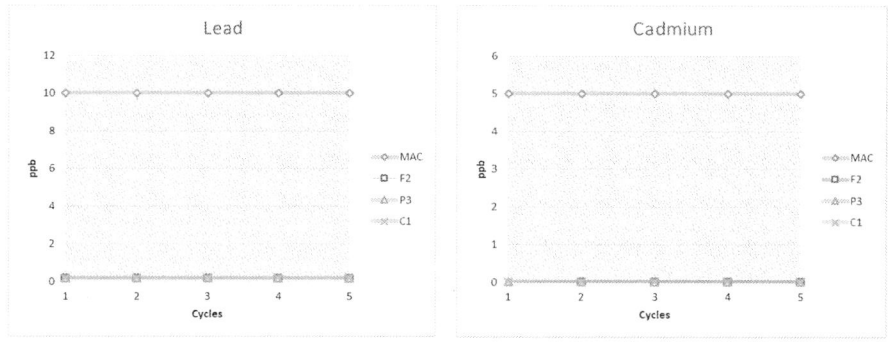

Figure 4. Migration tests for lead and cadmium levels

Porcelain enamel frits for hot water tanks are not made with lead, cadmium, or antimony. The migration test for these elements shows that these elements are not released into the drinking water in case they might be present in traces in the raw materials used to make the frit.

Conclusions

Porcelain enamel showed outstanding resistance to chemical attack of water at low and high temperatures and is suitable for contact with water for human consumption. Migration studies carried out by ICP and ICP/MS showed that the concentration of elements extracted on exposure to 85°C (185°C) hot water are always much lower the Maximum Allowed Concentration (MAC) of the parameters specified by DWD 98/83/CE. In this study the migration tests were carried out considering always the worst case in terms of test water quality (distilled was used) and correction factors (High S/V rate and high residence time).

Migration rates at lower temperatures of 25°C (77°F) and 65°C (149°F) are expected to be much lower than those at 85°C (185°F) per the Arrhenius equation:

$$M_n^T \approx e^{-Ea/RT}$$

where:

M_n^T = Migration rate at Absolute Temperature T
E_a = Activation Energy (70 kJ/mol)[12]
R = Gas Constant

and per prior knowledge of the enamelling technology.[12]

The results at 85°C (185°F) show migration well below the selected MAC values and no need of further migration tests at lower temperatures such as 25°C (77°F) and 65°C (149°F). The porcelain enamel migration study validated the proposed Positive Oxide Composition List (OCL). As such, the enamels falling within the OCL could be accepted for drinking water quality by means of the simplified approach of "AWT" Accepted Without Testing.

Appendix 1 – List of Acronyms Used

Acronym	Full Name
ACL	*Approved Constituent List for the European Acceptance Scheme*
ATP	Adenosine Tri-Phosphate
AoC	Attestation of Conformity; refers to the CPD system for attesting the conformity of construction products to European Technical Specifications
AWT-AWFT	Accepted Without Testing-Accepted Without Further Testing
CEN	Comité Européen de Normalisation (European Committee for Standardisation)
CL	Composition Lists for the European Acceptance Scheme
CPD	Construction Product Directive (Directive 89/106/EC)
CPDW	Construction Products in contact with Drinking Water
DG	Directorate General of European Commission
DWD	Drinking Water Directive (Directive 98/83/EC)
EAS	European Acceptance Scheme for CPDW
EC	European Commission
EFSA	European Food Safety Authority
EN	European Standard
EG-CPDW	Experts Group on CPDW
EOTA	European Organisation for Technical Approvals
EMG	Enhanced Microbial Growth
ETA	European Technical Approval
EU	European Union
FPC	Factory Production Control
GCMS	Gas Chromatography Mass Spectrometry – (analytical technique for identifying chemicals in leachates)
GNB	Group of Notified Bodies
hEN	harmonised European Standard
ITT	Initial Type Testing
MS	Member State of the EU
MTC	Maximum Tolerable Concentration
NAS	National Acceptance Scheme for construction products in contact with drinking water
NB	Notified Body (i.e. certification, inspection or testing bodies)
NCB	Notified Certification Body
NOAEL	No Observed Adverse Effect Level

NPD	No Performance Determined
NTL	Notified Testing Laboratory
OCL	Oxide Composition List of Vitreous Enamels for European Acceptance Scheme
PL	Positive List for the European Acceptance Scheme
RG-CPDW	Regulators Group on CPDW
RT	Residential Time
SCC	Standing Committee on Construction (CPD Article 19)
SCDW	Standing Committee on Drinking Water (DWD Article 12)
SCHER	Scientific Committee on Health and Environment Risks
SG1-OM	Experts Subgroup 1- Organic Materials
SG2-MM	Experts Subgroup 2 - Metallic Materials
SG3-NMIM	Experts Subgroup 3 - Non-Metallic Inorganic Materials (including Glassy Materials)
SG4-AMLP	Experts Subgroup 4- Assembled Multi-Layers Products
S/V	Surface vs. Volume Ratio
TC	Technical Committees of CEN
TDI	Tolerable Daily Intake
TOC	Total Organic Carbon
UAP	Unique Acceptance Procedure
WHO	World Health Organisation
CAS	Chemical Abstracts Service
EINECS	European Inventory of Existing Commercial Chemical Substances
p.p.b.	Parts per billion (equivalent to µg/L)
HWT	Hot Water Tank (= Water Heater = Boiler)
MAC	Maximum Allowed Concentration
M_n^T	Migration Rate at T°C for n^{th} period
HSM	Hot Stage Microscope
n.a.	not available
n.r.	not reported

Appendix 2 – List of Standard Test Procedures

UNI 6722	Vitreous Enamels: Inorganic Protective Coating - Determination of Resistance to Boiling Water and Water Vapour
UNI EN 1388-2	Material and Articles in Contact with Food Stuff - Silicate Surfaces - Determination of the Release of Lead and Cadmium from Silicates Surfaces other than Ceramic Ware
UNI 7232	Vitreous Enamels: Inorganic Protective Coating - Determination of Thermal Shock Resistance of Enamelled Cooking Utensils

UNI 7235	Vitreous Enamels: Inorganic Protective Coating - Production of Specimens of Sheet Steel
UNI 7674	Vitreous Enamels: Inorganic Protective Coating - Determination of Thermal Shock Resistance
UNI 8844	Vitreous and Porcelain Enamels - Determination of Release of Toxic Materials from Enamelled Ware in Contact with Food
UNI 1082-1	Vitreous and Porcelain Enamels: Guidelines for Design of Parts to be Enamelled
UNI 1082-2	Vitreous and Porcelain Enamels: Guidelines for the Design of Steel Boiler Intended to be Enamelled
UNI EN 89	Gas-Fired Storage Water Heater for the Production of Domestic Hot Water
UNI EN 14430	Vitreous and Porcelain Enamels: High Voltage Test
UNI EN 14483-1	Vitreous and Porcelain Enamels: Determination of Resistance to Chemical Corrosion. Part 1: Determination of Resistance to Chemical Corrosion by Acids at Room Temperature
UNI EN 14483-2	Vitreous and Porcelain Enamels: Determination of Resistance to Chemical Corrosion. Part 2: Determination of Resistance to Chemical Corrosion by Boiling Acids, Neutral Liquids and/or Their Vapours
UNI EN 14483-3	Vitreous and Porcelain Enamels: Determination of Resistance to Chemical Corrosion. Part 3: Determination of Resistance to Chemical Corrosion by Alkaline Liquids Using a Hexagonal Vessel
UNI EN 14483-4	Vitreous and Porcelain Enamels: Determination of Resistance to Chemical Corrosion. Part 4: Determination of Resistance to Chemical Corrosion by Alkaline Liquids Using a Cylindrical Vessel
UNI EN 14483-5	Vitreous and Porcelain Enamels: Determination of Resistance to Chemical Corrosion. Part 5: Determination of Resistance to Chemical Corrosion in Closed Systems
UNI EN ISO 8289	Vitreous and Porcelain Enamels: Low Voltage Test for Detecting and Locating Defects
UNI 9905	Vitreous Enamels: Inorganic Protective Coating for Hot Water Tanks, Standards and Testing
DIN 4753-3	Wassererwärmer und Wassererwärmungsanlangen für Trink-und Betriebswasser – Wasserseitiger Korrosionsschutz durch Emaillierung – Anforderung und Prüfung (Porcelain Enamel on Boilers and Water Heaters: Requirements and Tests)
EN 12873-1	Influence of Material on Water Intended for Human Consumption - Part 1: Test Method for Non-Metallic and Inorganic Materials for Factory-made Product
ISO 2722	Vitreous and Porcelain Enamels – Determination of Resistance to Citric Acid at Room Temperature
EN ISO 11885,	Water Quality — Determination of 33 elements by Inductively Coupled Plasma Atomic Emission Spectroscopy
EN 17294-2	Water Quality – Application of Inductively Coupled Plasma Mass Spectrometry (ICP-MS) – Part 2: Determination of 62 Elements

ISO 2733	Vitreous and Porcelain Enamels – Apparatus for Testing with Acid and Neutral Liquids and Their Vapours
ISO 2734	Vitreous and Porcelain Enamels – Apparatus for Testing with Alkaline Liquids
ISO 2744	Vitreous and Porcelain Enamels – Determination of Resistance to Boiling Water and Water Vapour
ISO 2746	Vitreous and Porcelain Enamels – Enamelled Articles for Service under Highly Corrosive Conditions - High Voltage Test
UNI EN ISO 8289	Vitreous and Porcelain Enamels – Low Voltage Test for Detecting and Locating Defects
D.M. 174/04	The regulation on materials and articles which can be used in collection, treatment, supply and distribution of water intended for human consumption
CPD 89/106/EEC	Construction Products Directive
DWD 98/83/CE	Council Directive on Quality of Water Intended for Human Consumption

Appendix 3 - Glossary

Accepted Without Further Testing (AWFT) - Product, material or constituent that has been tested and has been shown to be sufficiently below the limits in this EAS to be accepted without further testing. NOTE See text of EAS for criteria.

Accepted Without Testing (AWT) - Product or material that is accepted as being fit for use in contact with drinking water due to its composition and other requirements placed on the product/material, removing the need for testing of the finished product/material. NOTE This concept is applied to cementitious, glassy and metallic materials.

Assembled Product - These products comprise two or more components, possibly of different materials. Where the components are of different materials, it may be necessary to separately measure their impacts on water quality. This may require the product to be dismantled, but in some situations it will be proper to test the complete unit in its intended conditions of use.

Constituent - Ingredient used to make a material or product.

Material - Prepared form of a substance, or of a combination of substances, suitable for use in a manufacturing process.

Material Type - Category of materials of similar physical/chemical characteristics (e.g. organic, metallic, vitreous enamels).

Multi-Layer Product (Including Coatings) - Product made with more than one layer. Where there is a foreseeable possibility that the layers not initially intended to be in contact with water may, within the expected life of the product, eventually have an impact on water quality, each layer should be independently tested. (This situation might arise from migration through layers, or by the long-term deterioration of the layer intended to be in contact.) Where such an indirect action is not possible, e.g. because of the existence of a functional barrier (e.g., enamel), the layers that will not be in contact need not be tested.

Oxide Composition List - List of components/oxides that have been accepted for use in glassy or non-metallic inorganic products (vitreous enamels) with respect to toxicological, organoleptic, migration of metals and hygienic characteristics.

Product - Item made from a material or combination of materials or material types, in the form in which it is placed on the market.

Single Material Product - Product made with one single homogeneous material. Such products are relatively straightforward to test, using either the product itself, or a representative sample in the case of a large item.

Substance - Chemical or mixture of related chemicals used to make a material.

Vitreous/Porcelain Enamel - Borosilicate glassy structured material, whose chemical composition can be expressed only in terms of oxide composition and is almost insoluble in water because all elements are linked mainly with covalent chemical bonds. V.E./P.E. defined by EINECS N. 266-047-6 and CAS N. 65997-18-4.

Water Heater/Boiler/Hot Water Tank - Factory made product intended to produce and store hot water in buildings as a component of the indoor drinking water distribution system . The hot water is produced by means of electricity, gas or fuels and/or indirect exchange of hot fluids.

References

1. RG-CPDW 115: Comments concerning Enamelled Products
2. RG-CPDW 123: "Comparative Bacteriological Studies"
3. RG-CPDW 165: "Detailed Boiler Presentation"
4. CEN/TC164/WG3, document N 617: "WG3 Matrix"
5. EG-CPDW 200, 'RG-CPDW186 Final EAS
6. EG-CPDWD 223 'Glassy Material - EAS Approach Proposal I.E.I. Working Document".
7. Revised Mandate M 136 to CEN/CENELEC - Brussel, March,2006- G3 RK D(2005)
8. TG-CPDW 06-007 (RS 036 rev.5) "Accepted Without Testing / Without further Testing (draft) Procedural Aspects."
9. TG-CPDW 06 065A = TG DS 042A, Construct 06/763 "Construction Products in contact with Water intended for Human Consumption"
10. RG-CPDW 14 Rev.1 Coordinated DWD/CPD Glossary of Concepts & Tools for the EAS
11. Andrew I. Andrews – Porcelain Enamels – The Garrard Press, Publisher Champaign, Illinois, USA .
12. Lorenz R. – Mitt.des V.D.Efa, 1986, 34, 5, 65- Enamels for chemical Industry, corrosion by neutral water solutions.
13. EG-CPDW 238 rev.2, Glassy Materials/Porcelain-Vitreous Enamel Oxide Composition List (OCL) and Accepted Without Testing(ATW) approach in the framework of EAS of CPDW Directive- International Enamellers Institute (IEI) Working Document.
14. EG-CPDW_213_rev1- SGOM DOC 006
15. EG-cpdw_251 Annex II -v1 –table 11

Development of Durable Composites Incorporating Vitreous Enameled Metal

Charles A. Weiss, Jr., Paul G. Allison, Robert D. Moser, Brett A. Williams, Stacy S. Holton and Philip G. Malone
US Army Engineer Research and Development Center, Geotechnical and Structures Laboratory

Creating composites that are constructed from cemented media and metals provides some of the most useful construction materials that have been developed. Cementing systems such as concrete or organic polymers are used very effectively when combined with steel in a wide range of composite structures including conventionally-reinforced concrete, or metal fiber-filled polymer composites. In every composite involving metal, similar problems have to be addressed such as: 1) the cementing material and metal have to bond together so that stress can be shared between the materials, and 2) the metal cannot be allowed to corrode to the extent that the corrosion products produce debonding and unwanted stress on the composite. Advanced corrosion can also reduce the cross-sectional area of the reinforcing metal and weaken the composite. Vitreous or glass enamel is a very versatile coating to put on the surface of metal. It offers great protection from corrosion, and provides a surface that can be treated with coupling compounds like silanes or coated with a layer of reactive components that produce strong durable bonds when used in conjunction with the cementing phases. This report discusses the use of vitreous enamel coatings in producing durable metal-cement composites and examines the usefulness of adding or substituting enameled metal wire, rod or sheet. The glass-enameled metal could be of any desired size or shape and can be added to any other suitable reinforcing materials such as fiberglass mat or in certain cases the enameled metal can be the sole reinforcement. The new composite material can be an enameled metal reinforcement in concrete or polymer or even an enameled steel and fiberglass-polymer composite. The glass coating on the metal would be treated in a way similar to the glass fiber to assure that the bonding in an organic polymer matrix to the two materials is similar. The new composites could have some interesting applications where a strong, durable metal-reinforced version of fiber glass composite is needed.

Key words: fiberglass, enameled metal, bonding enamel, corrosion-resistance

INTRODUCTION
Vitreous Enamel Coatings Can Create New Composites

Vitreous enamel coatings on metals (especially on steel) are widely recognized as the most durable and strongly bonded coatings that can be put on metal[1]. However, the glass coating can also be useful as a bonding layer between metal and cementing phases that can be used to either create some useful composite that otherwise would not be possible or to improve the bonding in well-accepted composites such as reinforced concrete[2,3]. There are two strategies that can be used to improve bonds in composites. One involves taking advantage of the work that has been done on joining glass surfaces, such as silanes and polymer cements or specialized solder glass frits. The second involves adding a reactive ceramic to the surface of the enamel so that the reactive component can bond to the surrounding cement phases. Both approaches involve forming a well-bonded glass enamel layer on the metal.

ENAMELED STEEL IN ORGANIC CEMENT-BASED COMPOSITES
Polymer Coatings on Metal and on Glass Surfaces

Polymer coatings on steel are one of the most common methods of protecting steel from corrosion. There is a general loss of adhesion between the organic (epoxy) coatings and the surface of the steel if the coated (epoxy-painted or epoxy fused) metal is exposed to a moist environment, water, or high humidity. Investigations of the lower part of the epoxy layer have shown that there is a water layer that is many mono-layers thick and forms in the lower part of the epoxy layer and in the interface between the metal and the organic polymer layer[4]. This phenomenon occurs when any organic polymer bonded onto a high-energy substrate such as iron oxide is exposed to water or high relative humidity.[2] The surface of the iron is always covered by an iron oxide layer that is 3-4 nanometers thick that forms from contact with the air. The water layer is present at the organic coating-iron oxide interface because water molecules have a stronger affinity for the polar high energy iron oxide surface than does the organic film from the coating and therefore water molecules can displace the bonded organic film from the iron oxide substrate. The organic film-iron oxide affinity is only half of the estimated affinity of water molecules for the iron oxide film (<25 kJ/mol for the organic film compared to 40 to 60 kJ/mol). The vitreous enamel application replaces the iron oxide with a durable, tightly bonded, low-energy surface of silicate glass[4,5]. The silanes applied over the glass improve the affinity of the organic adhesive for the glass surface[6].

Research has begun to develop approaches to fabricating a new family of corrosion-resistant composites that use epoxy, glass fiber and enameled metal (for example, steel)[7]. The glass enamel coating should provide the metal with a surface that has the same characteristics chemically as a glass fiber. In effect, an enameled metal wire is conceptually a steel-reinforced, glass fiber and can be used in a mat of glass fibers, all embedded in a layer of organic polymer (epoxy). Also, the enamel prevents the steel from corroding. Any epoxy coating on metal would be more durable if it was applied over a silane-treated glass enamel that was fused onto the metal before the application of the silane and polymer.

Trials with an Enamel Steel Component in Fiberglass

The new composite would include a glass-enameled wire coated with a silane bonding-primer and embedded in a suitable epoxy. The wire component could be any metal that would take a vitreous enamel coating. The metals selection could include: mild steel, stainless steel, copper, brass, or aluminum. Also any metal that can be clad or plated with metals that can be enameled could be used. For the proof-of-concept work the team selected a mild steel that could be easily enameled. Lengths of mild steel wire (0.40-mm in diameter or 26 AWG) were cleaned and enameled. The wires selected were commonly available black annealed wire. A very active, tight-bonding base coat enameling system was used to produce a strong durable bond fusing the glass to the wire. A wide variety of suitable base-coat frits are available.

The wires to be enameled were pickled in a mild acid to remove the annealed coating. The wires were rinsed with clean water and dried. Glass frit was applied using a powder coating system but could also have been applied using electrophoresis, or a wet dip method. Any of the methods of applying the frit to the bare steel could be adapted for use with the wire. The frit used is a proprietary mixture, containing enameling glass and dispersing agents. The coated wires were fired between 800 and 850°C (1470 and 1560°F) for 3 to 4 minutes. The enameled samples of wire were handled without bending or deforming the metal. Samples of the un-enameled wire were cleaned but otherwise used in the condition in which they were received.

A wide variety of silane compounds are available for coating glass fiber for reinforcement in polymers. The silane selected for use in the first fabrication of a glass fiber-enameled metal composite was a commercial silane designed to have an organic reactivity with epoxy adhesives. This silane compound contains glycidoxy and methoxy groups and is especially useful in promoting adhesion to epoxies, and works with urethanes, acrylics and polysulfides. The silane used was a 3-glycidoxypropytrime-thoxysilane. It is widely used as a coating for glass fiber in fiberglass. It is also used as an embedding primer if the material is to be cast in a block of epoxy. The silane solution was used to coat the exterior surface of the enamel at full-strength as supplied.

A wide variety of epoxy compounds are used in making fiberglass. The epoxy components employed in this fabrication process are supplied in two syringes and a tubular in-line mixer is furnished so the uniformly mixed epoxy is dispensed and no additional mixing is required. The glass fabric used in the proof-of-concept work experimentation was a commercially available (6 ounce) woven glass cloth. The fibers in the glass cloth are precoated with silanes to provide a material that will saturate with and bond to epoxy. The cloth as furnished is approximately 4 mils thick.
Test samples were made by hand weaving the bare and the enameled 26 gauge wires into the woven glass fabric. Samples were made up from the bare un-enameled wire and the enameled wire. Both samples were cleaned with alcohol and coated with silane. The edges of the woven glass cloth were coated with a fast-setting ethyl cyanoacrylate glue to prevent unraveling. The samples were thoroughly dried at 80°C (175°F) and the center section was of each test specimen was impregnated with

epoxy. The epoxy was applied with a metering dispenser with an on-line mixer to assure that each sample had an identical injection of epoxy (Fig.1).

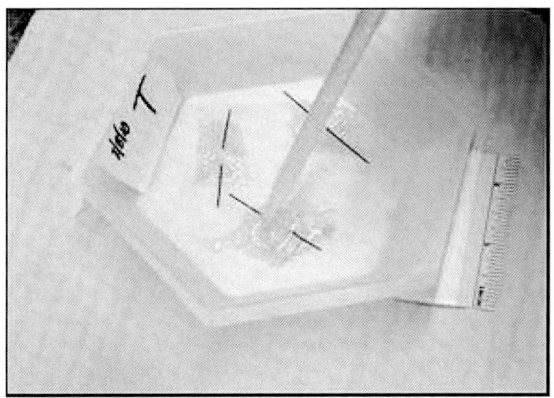

Fig. 1: Application of epoxy to the metal wire-glass fabric composite.

If the metal-glass composite was to be used in a similar way that fiber-glass would be used, the wire-glass fabric has to be stable. Without the enamel coating, the steel wire, even coated with epoxy, would rust. The enamel should be sufficient to protect the coated wire from corrosion and make it possible to expose the new metal reinforced fiber glass to a wet environment without the material corroding. Two batches of wire-reinforced fiberglass fabric were prepared in order to examine the benefits of using the enamel in making a practical steel and glass reinforced composite. The samples were then placed in a 100% humidity cabinet at 20°C (68°F) for 7 days.

Preliminary Examination of Hybrid Fiberglass Samples

Examination of the samples showed that the unenameled, silane-coated, and epoxy-embedded wire rusted and the corroded wire would not be useful for the new composite. The enameled and silane-coated wire embedded in epoxy was not corroded. Figure 2 shows the corroded and un-corroded wire samples in the glass fabric and epoxy composites.

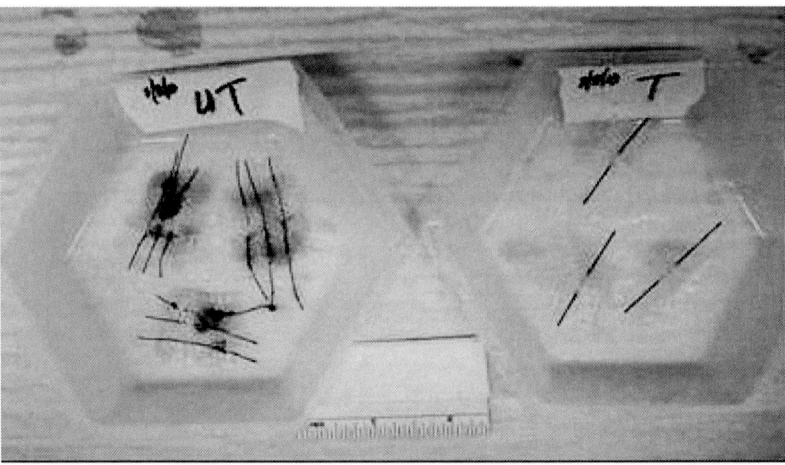

Fig. 2: Untreated wire (left) and treated wire (right) in glass fiber mat infiltrated with epoxy after 7-days exposure. The condition of the treated wire indicates it is possible to store and use the glass fabric wire composite just as the glass fabric with epoxy would be used.

A first look at the idea of using enameled wire as a substitute for glass fiber in a composite indicates that a durable enamel coating can be applied to steel wire using existing enameling frits and equipment that is currently in use in enameling production facilities. Normal enamel techniques can put a useful enamel coating on wire as thin as 0.40 mm (26 AWG). A 7-day corrosion test involving exposure to 100% humidity at 20°C (68°F) showed that the unenameled wire even in epoxy impregnated glass mat would rust. The enameled steel wire treated similarly remained free of corrosion. An application of a coupling compound, such as silane, the glass enameled steel bonded and exposure to moisture did not result in corrosion. Technically, a whole new group of composites that could be used for a variety of applications that had previous been the province of fiberglass only could be open to the new hybrid metal fiberglass composite. The new fiberglass composites consist of steel or even copper or aluminum either as the enameled metal alone or with glass fiber. Parts such as auto body panel or boat hulls could have integral metal reinforcement.

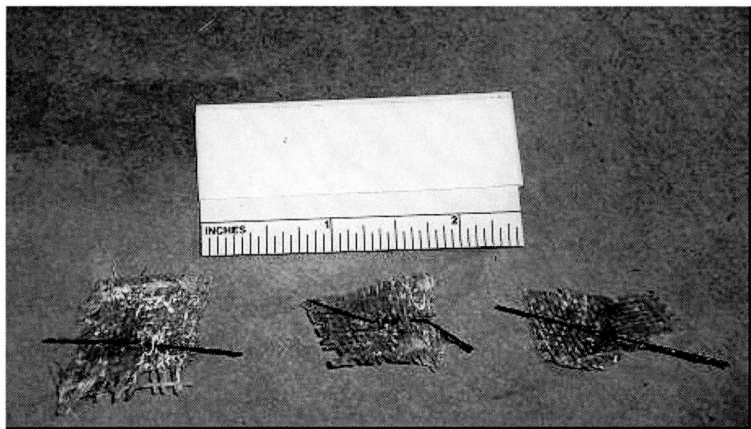

Fig. 3: Examples of composites made with silane-coated glass-enameled steel attached to epoxy-infiltrated glass fiber cloth.

Examination of the first samples of fiberglass-epoxy composite made with silated glass enamel indicated that there was no problem bonding the glass to the silane-treated enamel surface (Fig. 3). It would appear that this four-part composite does not have any compatibility problems. The experience with enameled metal indicates that the thermal expansion and contraction of most mild steel can be matched by the enameling glass. Glass fiber and epoxy typically have no thermal mismatches that would crack fiberglass. With the proper selection of materials, the new composite should be structurally sound over a wide range of conditions of temperature and moisture. The steel that would typically be the weak part of the system (due to its tendency to corrode) is protected by both the external epoxy and the glass enamel. Also this composite would appear to be superior to epoxy-over-bare-steel because there is no tendency for the glass enamel to delaminate from the steel. The flaw in epoxy coatings on steel has generally been the tendency for moisture or salt water to be drawn along between the epoxy layer and the surface of the steel. The glass can prevent this type of corrosion from developing.

Other Applications for this Technology

The metal-glass-silane and epoxy bonding system could be used to improve the durability of any bond where an organic polymer has to be permanently attached to metal. While presently it may not seem practical to enamel a steel part simply to attach a polymer handle or other fixture; enameling actually may provide the strongest and most durable bond. It may also be useful to consider making an enameled metal-glass cloth "sandwich" panel as a durable structural panel. A layer of enameled steel may be the easiest way of blocking ultra-violet light and ozone, the major environmental factors that degrade epoxy and other polymers.

ENAMELED STEEL IN INORGANIC CEMENT-BASED COMPOSITES

Patent applications on the use of a glass enamel that included a reactive vitreous coating were first filed by the Corps of Engineers in 2005[8] and subsequent studies have shown the coated rebar can produce improvements in bonding between rebar and conventional concrete that ranges from 5 to 10 times the normal bond strength between concrete and steel depending on the composition of the concrete and the curing conditions. Details on the production of coated steel using a two-coating enameling system are provided in Hackler[10]. Reactive enamel-coated steel has been produced for a wide range of application from continuously reinforced concrete pavements to steel fibers and wall ties for brick veneer wall construction. Tests with stay-in-place steel forms have shown that the composite of a coated steel shell and concrete infilling can produce a strong structural member that can handle higher loading and will have the corrosion-resistance to produce an improved service life[10].

The reactivity of the blended enamel coating indicates that enameled steel has a future application in newer cement formulations such as the geopolymer concretes that do not use conventional Portland cement[11]. Commercial pre-cast concrete production facilities are introducing geopolymer cements based on an alkali reaction with high aluminum-silica glasses found in fly ash from coal-fired power plants or in metallurgical slag. The use of waste products that replace all of the Portland cement in concrete has a promising economic future and has been cited as being a development to produce major environmental benefits by reducing carbon dioxide emissions and re-using waste material.

Investigations are currently underway on the use of reactive enamel-coated steel in these emerging geopolymer mortars and concretes. Initial testing indicates that steel pins prepared using the two-coating enameling system had 2.5 times stronger bond than the uncoated steel pins (Table 1). The geopolymer mortars are typically heat curing at 40 to 60°C (104 to 140°F) and can have a strength of 60 to 70 MPa (9,000 to 10,000 psi) in seven days depending on the formulation of the concrete. The reactive enamel-coated steel reaches bond strength that is 1.8 times that of bare steel with curing times as short as 7 days and increases with additional curing. At 28 days the coated steel has bond strengths that are 2.5 times that of uncoated steel. Photomicrographs with elemental mapping (Fig. 4) indicate the transition from the two-layered enamel to the surrounding hardened geopolymer and the transition from the bare metal to the geopolymer.

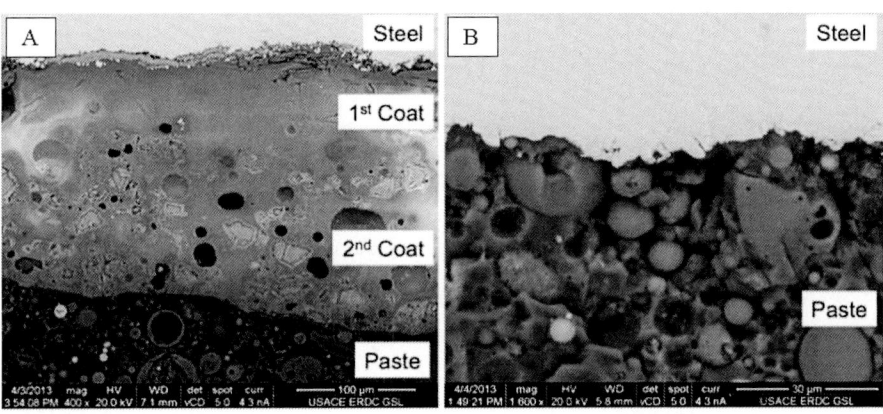

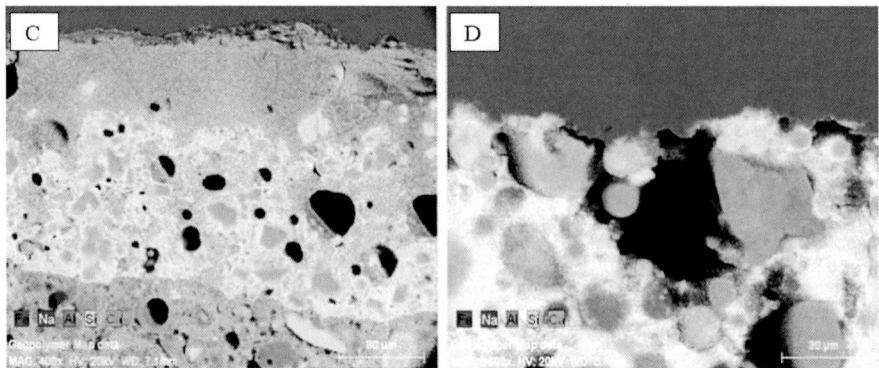

Fig. 4: Interface between reactive vitreous enamel and surrounding geopolymer.
  A. Photomicrograph of polished section of coated steel in geopolymer
  B. Photomicrograph of polished section of uncoated steel in geopolymer
  C. Elemental map produced from polished section of coated steel in geopolymer
  D. Elemental map produced from polished section of uncoated steel in geopolymer

Surface Treatment	Curing Time (days)	Average Bond Strength, MPa (psi)	Std. Dev. MPa (psi)
Enameled	3	14.84 (2152.4)	2.79 (404.7)
Bare Steel	3	8.11 (1176.2)	2.16 (313.3)
Enameled	7	16.17 (2345.3)	5.14 (745.5)
Bare Steel	7	7.04 (1021.1)	1.46 (211.8)
Enameled	28	12.28 (1781.1)	2.74 (397.4)
Bare Steel	28	4.90 (710.7)	1.14 (165.3)

Table 1. Bond Strengths of Vitreous Coated and Uncoated Steel Pins Embedded in Geopolymer Mortar

The initial successes with a bonding enamel formulated with calcium silicates suggest that the development of high aluminum-silica glasses that are compatible with fly ash glass may produce even better bonding. The outer layer could be designed to rapidly react with the alkali-activator solution and produce a strong transition from a geopolymer gel to a layer of alkali-reactive aluminum-silica glass that is fused to a durable enameling glass.

SUMMARY

Specialized glass enamels can be useful in a wide variety of composite materials. The enameling glasses can bond well to a variety of metals. Unlike bare metal surfaces water and corrosion effects are excluded. The use of glass with organic polymers offers some unusual possibilities for developing a new group of strong versatile fiberglass-like composites. Using enameled metal embedded with epoxy presents an unusual composite where the glass can prevent debonding and the protection from the metal can prevent ozone and ultraviolet light from degrading the organic polymer.

The use of bond enamel on steel reinforcement has expanded into a variety of new application such as corrosion-proof, strong bonding wall ties, coated steel fibers and continuous sheet metal reinforcement in conventional concrete. New designs for reinforcement can take advantage of the bond strength and the corrosion protection the enameled steel can provide.

Enameled steel reinforcement can develop along with alkali-activated or geopolymer cement and concrete. Since geopolymer is a product of alkali-reaction with aluminum-silica rich waste glasses (fly ash or slag) the use of a specially formulated enameling system appears to be a very useful transition from the surface of the metal to the surrounding aluminosilicate gel. Successes with a bonding enamel formulated with calcium silicates suggest that the development of high aluminum-silica glasses that are compatible with fly ash glass may produce even better bonding. Geopolymer is particularly suited to manufacture of pre-cast concrete items (culvert, concrete pipe, etc.). Pre-formed rebar cages designed for enameling could make assembly and casting for utility boxes and jersey barrier a rapid method of production for a greatly improved product.

ACKNOWLEDGEMENTS

The authors wish to recognize the efforts of Linda J. Ragan and Erin Rae Gore in developing and analyzing data for this report.

REFERENCES

1. F. Shieu, K-C. Lin and J-C. Wong. "Microstructure and Adherence of Porcelain Enamel and Low Carbon Steel." Ceramics Intern. 25 (1999) p. 27.

2. C. Hackler. "Technical Advances in Reactive Vitreous Enamels for Reinforcing Steel in Concrete Structures," 22nd International Enamellers Congress (2012). Cologne, Germany.

3. C. Hackler, M. Koenigstein and P. Malone. "The Use of Porcelain Enamel Coatings on Reinforcing Steel to Enhance the Bond to Concrete." Materials Science and Technology Conf. and Exhibition, Conference Proceeding (2006). Amer. Ceramic Soc. Westerville, OH.

4. T. Nguyen, and J. Martin, 1996. Modes and Mechanisms of Degradation of Epoxy-coated Reinforcing Steel in a Marine Environment. in C. Sjostrom, C. (ed.) Durability of Building Materials and Components (Volume 1) E &FN Spon, London.

5. T. Nguyen, E. Byrd, and D. Bentz. "A Study of Water at the Coating/Substrate Interface." Jour. of Coatings Tech. 66 (1994) p. 39.

6. S. Feldman, and C. Baldwin, "Surface Tension and Fusion Properties of Porcelain Enamels, "Proceedings of the 69th Porcelain Enamel Inst. Tech. Forum, (Alpharetta, GA: PEI, 2008) p. 1-10.

7. S. Morefield, C. Weiss, Jr., P. Malone and M. Koenigstein. "Design of Corrosion-Resistant Composites Incorporating Vitreous Enameled Metal.". (2011).
https://www.corrdefense.com/Spotlight/2011%20Corrosion%20Conference%20Presentations/Design%20of%20Corrosion-resistant%20com-

posites%20incorporating%20vitreous%20enameled%20metal.pdf

8. E. P. Plueddemann, "Silane Coupling Agents." Second Edition (1991) Springer-Verlag, New York.

9. U.S. Patent Office. "System and Method for Increasing the Bond Strength Between a Structural Material and Its Reinforcement" by Sykes et al., ser. no. 11/234,184, filed: September 26, 2005.

10. C. Hackler. "Improving Steel-Reinforced Concrete Structures." Ceramic Industry,
May 1, 2010. http://www.ceramicindustry.com/articles/print/improving-steel-reinforced-concrete-structures.

11. Federal Highway Administration. "Geopolymer Concrete." (2010) Publ. No. FHWA-HIF-014, Washington, DC.

Challenges and Outlook for Key Raw Materials

Mark Doak, Patrick Palattella, Charles Baldwin
Ferro Corporation

The 2000s commodities boom caused by rising demand from emerging markets caused sharp increases in the costs of many raw materials. The Great Recession offered some relief from the trend, but other unprecedented raw material cost increases and/or volatility have occurred since with materials such as rare earths, titania, and zircon. The raw material cost increases, re-formulation efforts undertaken by Ferro, and the outlook for select raw materials are reviewed.

The basic component of porcelain enamel coatings is glass frit. The great majority of the formulations are based on alkali borosilicate but with additions that cover the whole periodic table for every non-toxic cost-competitive oxide. As such, up to 40 raw materials are required for frit making. This paper focuses on key recently financially challenging raw materials:

1. Cobalt Oxide
2. Nickel Oxide
3. Titanium Dioxide
4. Zirconium Silicate (Zircon)
5. Lithium Carbonate
6. Cerium Oxide

The volatility of cobalt through the decades is well known in the enamel industry, but all six materials have had periods of scarcity and price spikes.[1] Analysis of the reaction of the industry to changes in the scarcity of these raw materials requires an understanding of price elasticity. Prices are elastic if substitutes are available. So, as the price increases, less is used, alternate materials are used, or recycled feedstocks become a more significant source of the material. When substitutes start to be used, manufacturers purchase less of the scarce raw material. This causes demand destruction, which is decreased demand for the scarce raw material because of the use of substitutes. If prices are inelastic, substitutes are not readily available. Price increases push higher extraction cost reserves into production, which adds to capacity and can eventually stabilize the price.[2]

Ferro Corporation procurement continually monitors raw material trends. Reformulation is done if required and feasible, but porcelain enamel coatings must continue to meet applicator requirements. The formulator and the business need to be aware of the risks and trade-offs of oxide reduction and raw material substitution.

1. **Cobalt Oxide**

Cobalt oxide is used up to a few weight percent in porcelain enamels as well as glass in general as a blue coloring agent. It is critical to porcelain enamels (often in combination with nickel and, to a lesser degree, iron, manganese, and copper) to create adherence of ground coats to steel.[3] Cobalt was originally used centuries ago as a strong blue pigment for stained glass cathedral windows, Persian ceramics, and Chinese dinnerware. The name "Cobalt" originated from the German word Kobold for goblin, due to superstitions by medieval miners who had to suffer from arsenic fumes from roasting cobalt-containing smaltite ore from Saxony.[4] In modern times, cobalt is a by-product of copper mining, with half of the sources within the Democratic Republic of the Congo (DRC) in Central Africa. World production of cobalt was over 80,000 MT in 2011 and increasing.[5] The diverse uses of cobalt outside of porcelain enameling found in commercial, industrial, and military applications are shown in Figure 1. The leading use of cobalt is currently in rechargeable battery electrodes followed by superalloys, which are metal alloys with excellent mechanical strength, high-temperature creep resistance, and corrosion resistance and are often used in gas turbine engines.

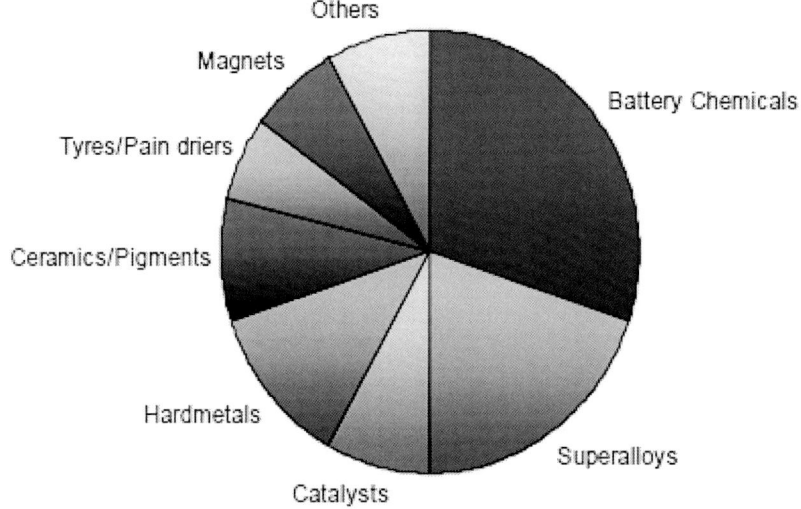

Figure 1. Uses of cobalt

As shown in Figure 2, cobalt prices have been historically volatile. In 1978, the price increased over 300% from $6/lb ($13/kg) to $25/lb ($55/kg) (in 1978 dollars) in less than one year due to political unrest in what is now the Katanga Province in the DRC (then Zaire). Responses included stockpiling, a search for substitutes, re-activation of old US mines, and increased use of reclaiming spent catalysts as secondary production. The porcelain enamel industry worked frantically and proactively to replace the cobalt in ground coats with nickel, and blue enamels were replaced with gray ones.[6] By 1981, demand destruction from substitutes and availability of cobalt from outside Zaire had dropped Zaire's US market share from 70% to 26%, and price had dropped significantly by 1982.[7] The price stayed in line with long term trends until the early 1990s. Speculative price levels of $25/lb ($55/kg) (1992 dollars) in 1992 created another round of substitution efforts, which tapered off when soft economic conditions in the early 1990s reduced demand. From 1995 to 2002, prices steadily fell from $27/lb to $6/lb.

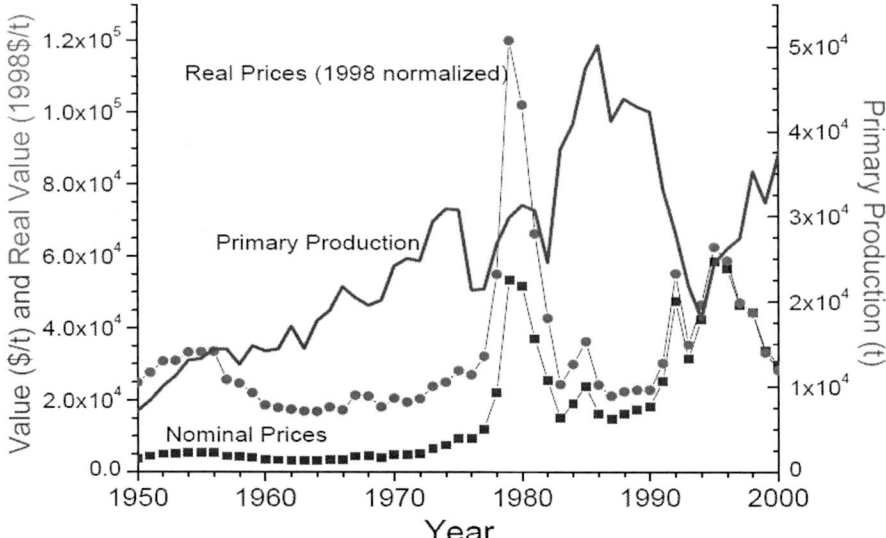

Figure 2. Cobalt market price, 1950 to 2000, versus production[8]

From 2002 to 2008, prices escalated sharply and peaked at $50/lb in March 2008 (shown in Figure 3) because of the emergence of China as a major refined cobalt producer and consumer. The combination of new sources coming on-line to satisfy Chinese demand and the impact of the Great Recession caused cobalt prices to fall dramatically to $11/lb in December 2008. Since then, prices rebounded somewhat but settled back to $11/lb.

Challenges and Outlook for Key Raw Materials

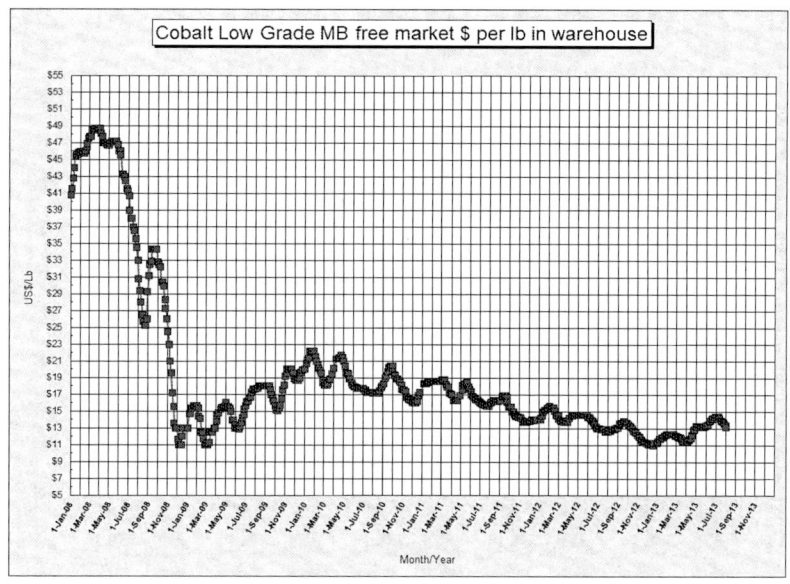

Figure 3. Cobalt market 2008 to Present

Higher prices have driven increases in production. As shown in Figure 4, cobalt production from all regions has increased from about 25,000 MT/year in 1995 to 70,000 MT/year in 2008 because of increasing demand. Cobalt production from the DRC increased to 41% from 7%, Zambia decreased to 9% from 24%, Canada decreased to 11% from 22%, and Russia decreased to 8% from 14%. While China has significantly increased its cobalt refining capacity, its mined capacity remained no higher than 9%, making China reliant on imports.

Challenges and Outlook for Key Raw Materials

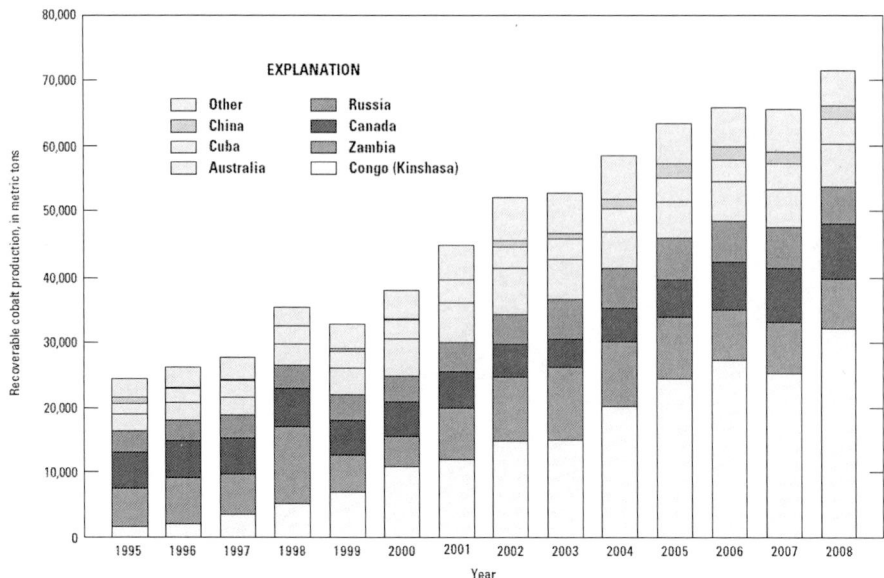

Figure 4. Principal sources of recoverable cobalt[9]

The high cobalt prices that lasted until 2008 also drove an increase in expected secondary sourcing from by-products of precious metal mining, shown in Figure 5.

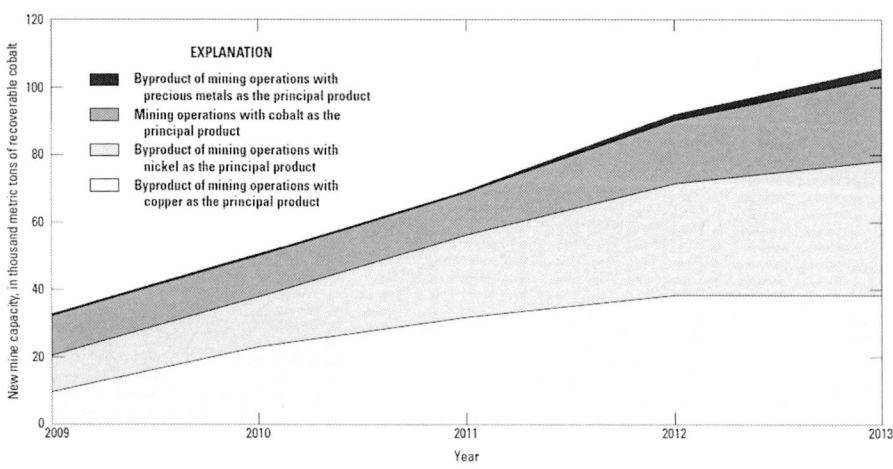

Figure 5. Anticipated cobalt capacity, 2009 to 2013

The increased production from the high prices during the commodity boom has created an ample supply for the moment. Batteries are not putting undue pressure on cobalt because nickel/manganese can be substituted. Cobalt is a function of copper demand, which is directly proportional to the amount of global economic growth, which has been sluggish with Asia relatively slow, the US in a slow recovery, and Europe hurt by the debt crisis. This would suggest pricing stability, but the unknown factor is political unrest in central Africa. The government of the DRC would like to see more mining revenue stay in the country. During 2013, an export quota requiring more refining in the country was suggested and briefly pushed up prices. An increased export tax was levied instead[10], but enamelers need to be watchful of the situation.

2. **Nickel**

Nickel is used with cobalt to create adhesion and refire bond strength. Nickel and cobalt can roughly be interchanged for adhesion in ground coats with color shifts from nickel's brown to cobalt's blue. During the 1978 cobalt crisis, nickel was the primary substitute for cobalt.[11] New REACH regulations in Europe have led to nickel elimination from ground coats, making any future cobalt replacement with nickel impossible in that market.[12] Instead of substitution, cobalt or nickel can be reduced, but care should be taken to maintain acceptable bond to steel as measured by impact adhesion tests such as ASTM B916.

Sulfide and laterite ores are the two main sources for primary nickel. Laterite ores containing nickeliferous limonite [$(Fe,Ni)O(OH)$] and garnierite (hydrous nickel silicate) are generally found in the tropics. These are exposed with time in layers by weathering. Sulfide ores containing pentlandite [$(Ni,Fe)_9S_8$] are usually found underground in conjunction with copper.[13] The sulfide is roasted to form the oxide used in frit making.

Austenitic stainless steel accounts for about 65% of the nickel consumed, followed by 12% for superalloys and nonferrous alloys for aerospace and turbine applications. The remaining 23% is used in alloy steels, rechargeable batteries, catalysts, nickel-containing chemicals, coinage, foundry products, and plating.[14] The nickel market since 2008 is shown in Figure 6. Like cobalt, the nickel market was very tight until the collapse of demand with the onset of the Great Recession in late 2008. Since then, China is the largest user of stainless steel, and the slowing of their economy has caused nickel to tumble to the lowest level in the past two years. The future price is uncertain and will depend on stainless steel demand.

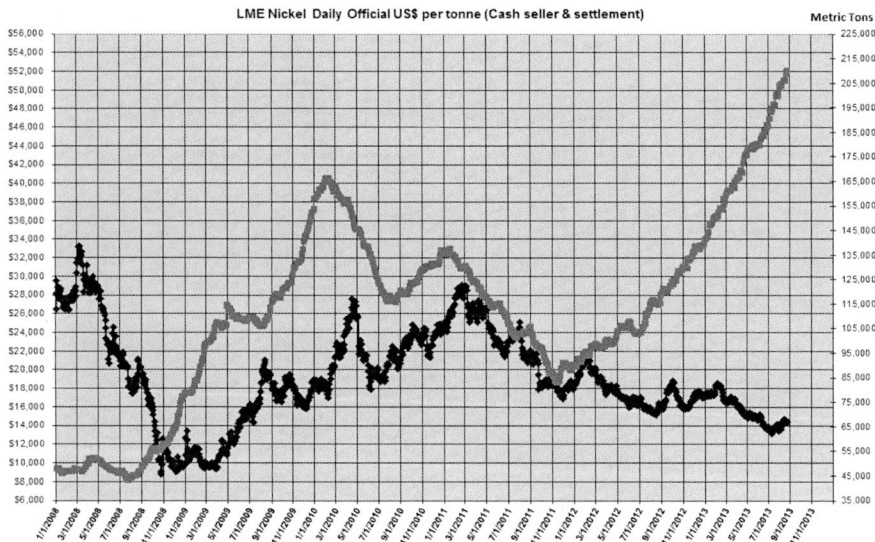

Figure 6. Nickel market, 2008 to Present

3. **Zirconium Silicate**

Zircon ($ZrSiO_4$) melted into frit adds alkali and water resistance to enamels by adding zirconium dioxide "zirconia" (ZrO_2) to the glass. Mill added zirconia imparts some opacity to ground coats. Zircon is obtained from mining and processing heavy mineral sands ore deposits that are also used as sources of titanium minerals, ilmenite, rutile, and tin.[15] Zircon is used for refractories, foundry sands, and ceramics. Ceramics include porcelain enamels as well as the larger usage for floor and roof tile. Zirconium metal is used in nuclear reactors, corrosion-resistant chemical piping, heat exchangers, and specialty alloys.

Shown in Figure 7, the cost of zircon sharply rose in 2010. The large price run up was initially a supply and demand imbalance, particularly from the Chinese refractory industry. As this demand caused a short term shortage, some suppliers became predatory and helped in the run up, so a part of this inflated price was artificial. As the pricing continued to climb, many that could switch did so. Those that could not were subject to the higher pricing, as all suppliers were matching these higher prices. In late Q3 2012, the bottom fell out of the market. Many say that the demand in China fell way off. Others point to the large oversupply from the mines. As shown in Figure 7, the market price dropped from $2,600/MT down to $2,000/MT. This has continued to diminish in subsequent auctions and is now down to a low nearing $1,000/MT very recently in Asia.

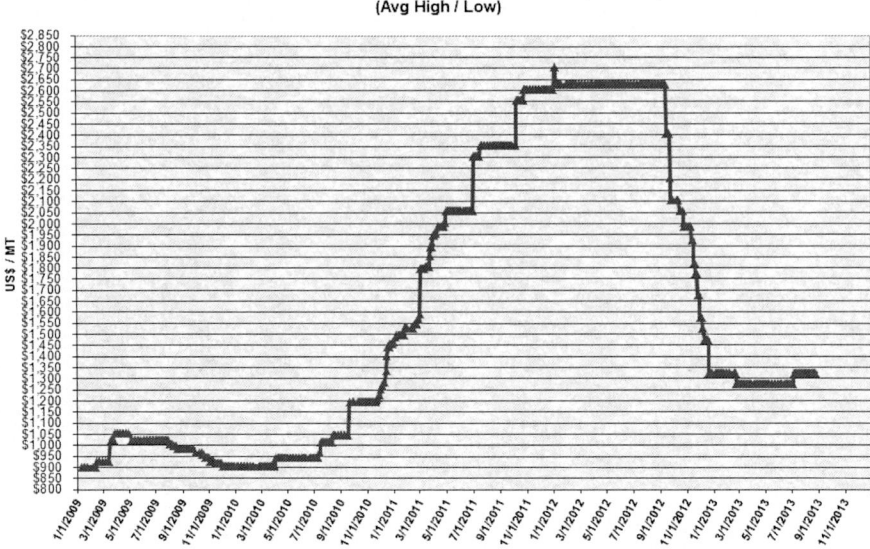

Figure 7. Zircon sand market, 2009 to Present

For the outlook for zircon cost, many suppliers have acknowledged this excess inventory and are saying that it is just about gone. Some say the Chinese demand is coming back, where others do not see that. Despite the mixed opinions, the bottom line is that the pricing has potentially reached bottom and may start to increase in the short to medium term. However this increase should not be anything like the last run up or at least not until the Chinese market rebounds.

To test the ability to replace the zircon in ground coat, an alkali-resistant ground coat formulation was smelted in the lab with the original zircon level, 50% less, and 0%. The frit was milled into a dry electrostatic system, sprayed, and fired. The enamel coating was tested for weight loss after 6 hours exposure to boiling 6% sodium tetrapyrophosphate solution. The results shown in Figure 8 versus the customer weight loss specification of 5 mg/in^2 show that zircon can be reduced, but some zircon is required to meet customer specifications.

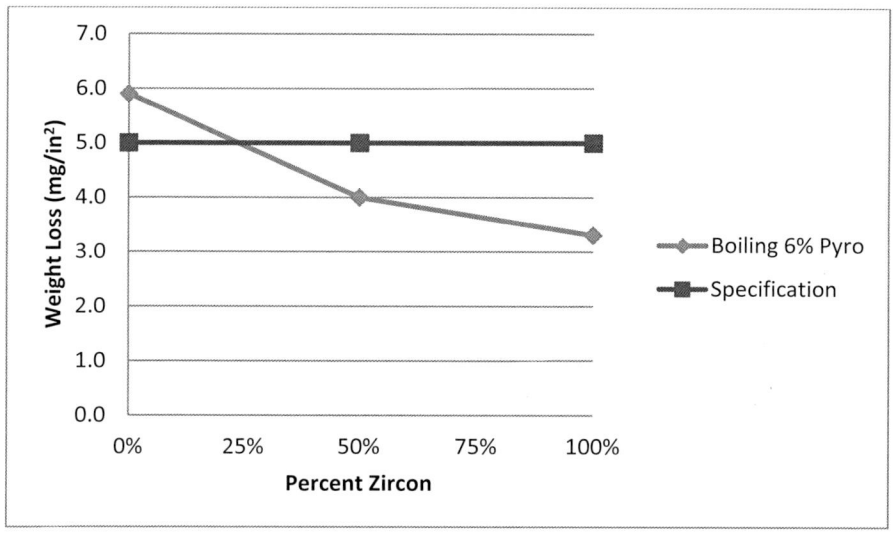

Figure 8. Effect of zircon reduction on alkali resistance

4. Titanium Dioxide

Titanium dioxide is a white material with a very high refractive index so it readily lends itself to use as an opacifier for paints and porcelain enamels. Titanium white enamels depend on recrystallization of titanium dioxide from supersaturated glass and were first developed in the 1950s. The two polymorphic forms used and found in porcelain enamel are anatase and rutile. Rutile has a tetragonal crystalline structure with a space group of P 4/mnm,[16] while anatase is also tetragonal but with space group $I4_1/amd$[17]. Rutile has an index of refraction of 2.616 to 2.903 compared to 2.488 to 2.560 for anatase.[18] Titanium dioxide is produced either by digesting ilmenite ore in sulfuric acid to remove the iron followed by purification and calcination, or through the chlorination of rutile ore to form titanium tetrachloride that is then purified, vaporized, and oxidized.[19] The same mineral sands used as sources of titanium dioxide are also sources of zircon.

In 2007, titanium dioxide was a $10.5 billion dollar market split roughly equally between North America, Europe, and Asia. The major applications are for pigment for architectural and automotive paint, plastics, and paper.[20] Recrystallized anatase titania provides white in cover coats at a level of 15 to 20% dissolved into the frit. Rutile is used for acid resistance in ground coat enamels.

Titanium dioxide prices rose up to 60 to 70% during 2010-2011 from increased straining capacity reductions made during the economic crisis. Both anatase and rutile prices have increased. Recently, there has been a slight softening in the market but prices have not returned to previous levels, and titania producers are still seeking increases.

To explore substitution options to use more of the slightly lower cost rutile than anatase, 0, 25, 50, 75, and 100% of anatase was replaced with rutile in the raw batch of a full titanium white cover coat. The frit was smelted in the lab, milled wet, and fired. Color was measured versus 100% anatase standard enamel. The results in Figure 9 show a significant shift yellower. Contaminants such as iron, chromium, and vanadium in rutile flour prevent its use in white cover coats. Therefore, anatase is required for appliance white colors.

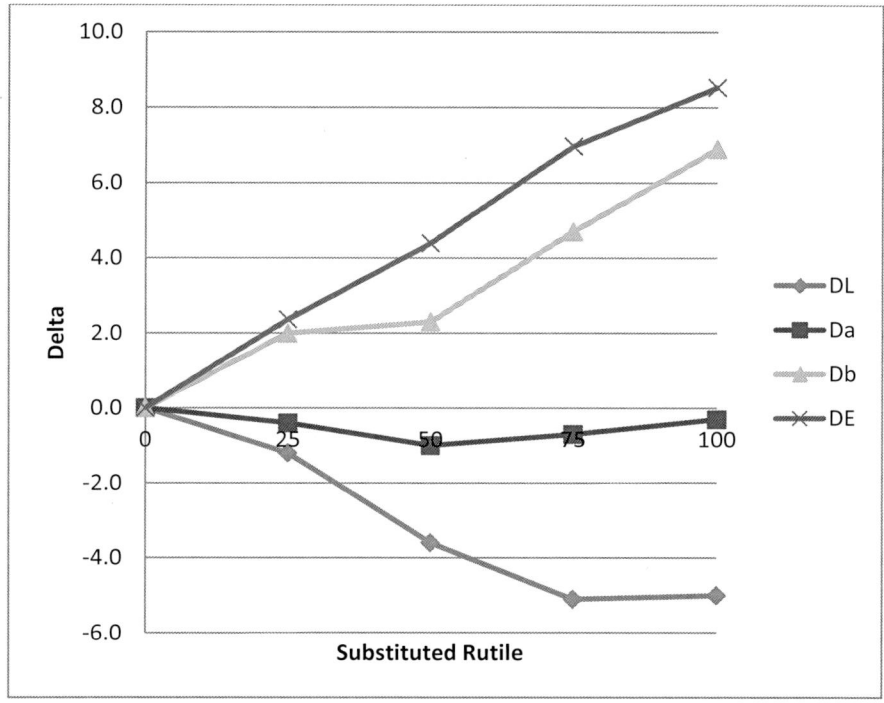

Figure 9. Effect of rutile substitution on white cover coat color

The alternative to substitution is reduction of a scarce raw material. The titanium dioxide level was reduced in a wet white cover coat frit by 13%. The fired enamel made from the frit was able to meet color requirements of 89 opacity at full application. However, as shown in Figure 10, coverage was reduced. This would lead to potentially more light spray defects in mass production. Other modifications to the glass to force the same recrystallization at lower titania level could have other trade-offs like color stability and loss of acid resistance.

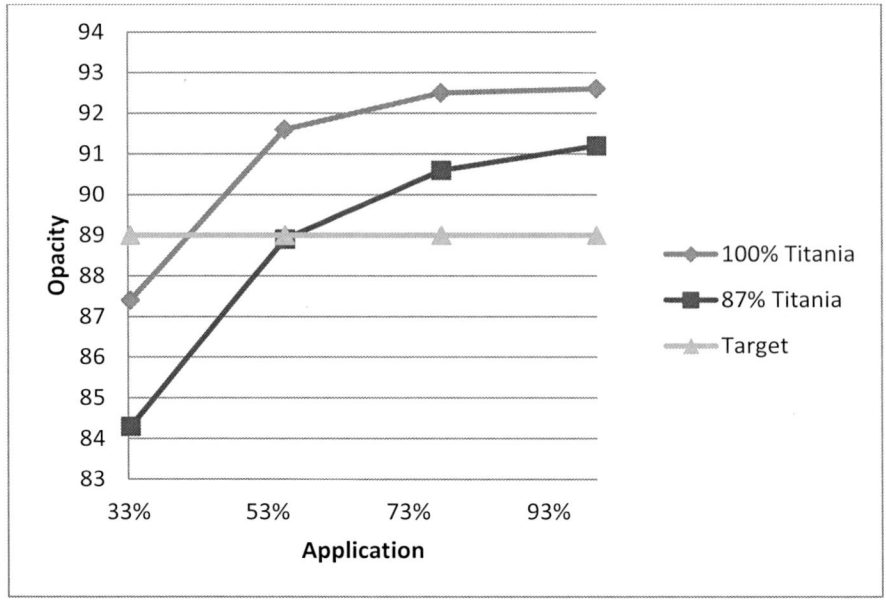

Figure 10. Effect of titania reduction on coverage

5. **Lithium**

The leading application of lithium according to the US Geological Survey (USGS) is 30% as a flux in ceramics and glass, but its second most common use as a component of high energy-density rechargeable lithium ion batteries is the most valuable.[21] Lithium is preferred because of its high charge-to-weight ratio. Compact, lightweight lithium ion batteries have been key to the revolution in smartphones, tablet computers, and laptop computers; by 2002, 95% of cell phones had lithium ion batteries.[22] Lithium production increased from about 8,000 MT/year in 1990 to about 25,000 MT/year in 2008. Lithium ion batteries are already used in commercially-available electric automobiles (EVs) and are being explored for power storage from wind turbines and solar panels. Any significant adoption of EVs by consumers has the potential to seriously strain the available lithium supply.[23]

Capacity, particularly for lithium carbonate, has not grown fast enough to keep up with growing demand for batteries. Eighty-seven percent of lithium reserves are in brine deposits at salt flats, predominately located at the Salar de Atacama in Chile, the Salar del Hombre Muerto in Argentina, and the Salar de Uyuni in Bolivia along with deposits in China. The Salar de Uyuni in Bolivia has no current production, but is estimated to hold up to 50% of the world's lithium reserves. Lithium can also be obtained by mining spodumene (lithium aluminosilicate). In enamel frits, lithium is used as a flux and, with sodium and potassium, provides optimal dry electrostatic application. For frit making, spodumene has a lower lithium yield, and also yields aluminum oxide that is detrimental to acid resistance.

Lithium is already established as a new green energy source for battery cathodes that also contain cobalt or nickel. Battery demand was foreseen in a 1974 PEI paper when the automotive industry was pushing battery research in response to the 1970s energy crisis.[24] The current lithium capacity is insufficient to supply rapidly growing demand so price is steadily increasing. There are potential supply concerns although more reserves are available. The amount of future demand will depend on the electric automobiles produced and how much lithium is used for power storage. Producers are not concerned about demand destruction from price escalation. The forecast is for increasing cost, and the level will depend on rate of increase of battery production versus lithium production as well as the rate of recovering lithium and metal oxides through battery recycling.

The substitutes in frit are sodium and potassium. Lithium reduction/substitution has potential negative impacts on frit fluidity and thermal expansion. Lithium reduction tends to negatively impact bond from changes to the enamel viscosity above the glass temperature. Also, the use of spodumene adds aluminum oxide that degrades acid resistance. For electrostatic powders, an optimal balance of lithium, sodium, and potassium is required for optimal transfer properties. It is possible to make modest reductions with acceptable performance trade-offs, but elimination is impossible.

6. **Rare Earths**

Cerium oxide is the rare earth oxide most commonly used in porcelain enamels. The rare earths, or lanthanides, are the first set of elements from lanthanum (atomic number 57) to lutetium (atomic number 71) on the periodic table with filled f electronic orbitals. The lanthanides are not actually that "rare". Lanthanum, cerium, and neodymium are more common in the earth than lead.[25]

Cerium is used as a polishing compound for hard drive platters and electronics, as a catalyst, and as a smelted-in opacifier in porcelain enamel. It is more stable than titanium dioxide under reducing conditions, and does not interfere with enamel adhesion.

In the second half of 2010, the People's Republic of China cut rare earth exports 70%. While there are rare earth deposits at Mountain Pass in California, extraction had stopped well before 2010 because of cost and environmental concerns. That left the overwhelming majority of rare earth production in China. This also included scarcer rare earths used in modern electronics, smartphones, hard drives, and televisions. As shown in Figure 11, the export quota reduction sent the cost of the rare earth oxides skyrocketing but was initially absorbed while reformulation efforts started. In 2011, cerium was reclassified by China as a light rare earth and the export quota was changed. The cerium cost has fallen significantly since then from the reclassification as well as from demand destruction.

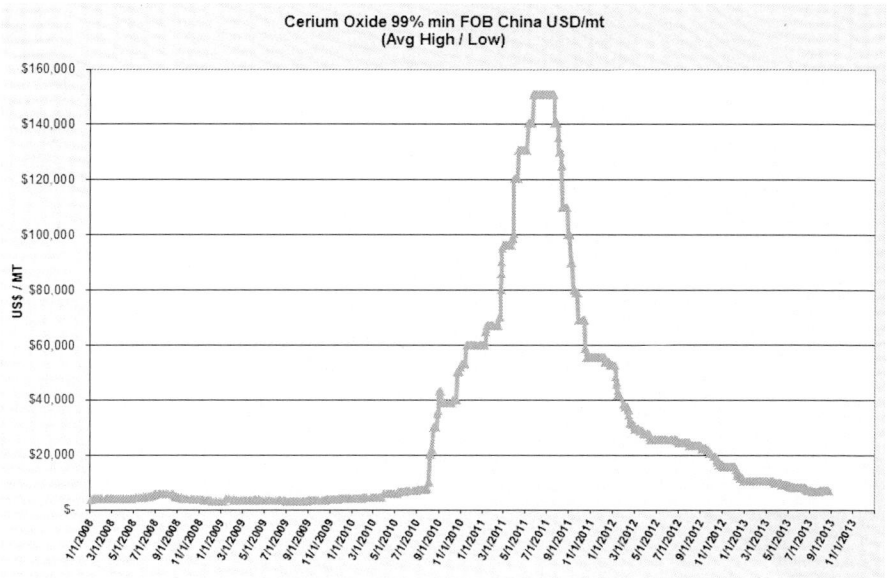

Figure 11. Cerium market, 2008 to Present

An example of demand destruction in enamels was the complete replacement of cerium as an opacifier in Ferro's Evolution® product line.[26] For that frit, the alternate opacifier gave similar color and met application requirements. Cerium is used for solid gray colored ground coats. Replacement was explored using zirconium dioxide as a substitute opacifier. As shown in Figure 12, the change in opacity with increasingly high temperature fire changed dramatically when zirconia was used. Cerium oxide resulted in a very color-stable gray ground coat. Zirconia could be used to match the color at 1520°F, but was four points dark at 1570°F. Therefore, cerium is needed to be able to produce color stable enamel.

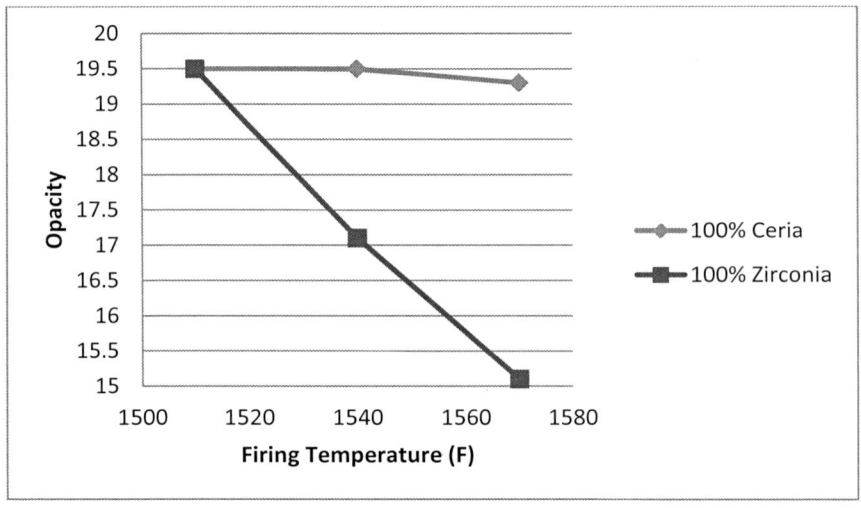

Figure 12. Effect of replacing cerium with zirconia opacifier

Summary

The sources, major uses and market conditions were reviewed for cobalt, nickel, zircon, anatase titanium dioxide, lithium, and cerium. Increasing demand for batteries is putting pressure on cobalt, nickel, and lithium. Cobalt and nickel have more substitutes in batteries, but lithium is particularly inelastic. Zircon and titania are both connected to the demand for mineral sands. Table 1 summarizes the outlook and substitution options of each.

Raw Material	Outlook	Substitution/Reduction Options
Cobalt	Flat	Nickel, not in Europe
Nickel	Uncertain	Substitute cobalt
Zircon	Down to previous levels	Modestly reduce
Titania (Anatase)	Slightly up	Difficult to reduce
Lithium	Up	Modestly reduce
Cerium	Slightly up	Reduce

Table 1. Porcelain enamel key raw materials outlook and elasticity

The risks and tradeoffs of substitution of the raw materials in porcelain enamels were reviewed. First, nickel can and has been used to replace cobalt. Unfortunately, this is no longer an option in the European market because of REACH regulations restricting nickel. Reduction of cobalt or nickel has the risk of reducing enamel bond. The outlook for cobalt is flat as long as there is not a disruption in African sources. Second, the nickel outlook strongly depends on the amount of stainless steel production, particularly in Asia. Third, reducing zircon negatively impacts the chemical resistance. Zircon is expected to return to previously levels. Fourth, anatase titanium dioxide is required for bright white colors, and it is expected to move slightly upwards in cost. Replacement with rutile shifts colors darker and yellower. Reducing anatase reduces coverage. Fifth, lithium is a strong flux that provides optimal bond, color, thermal expansion, and electrostatic transfer properties. It can be reduced modestly but not eliminated and is expected to continue moving upwards in price. The trajectory will depend on the rate of adoption of lithium ion batteries in transportation. Finally, cerium usage can be reduced but not eliminated for all formulations. It should be stable to slightly up since reclassification as a light rare earth.

Example lab work showed drastic reductions in critical raw materials in a frit will cause significant loss in enamel performance. Modest balanced reductions have been made, approved by applicators, and fully commercialized. Ferro has done this for products such as pyrolytic ground coats, sanitaryware ground coat, cookware ground coat, cast iron enamels, and Evolution® cover coats. Ferro will also continue to monitor raw material trends and reformulate accordingly to provide optimal products meeting customer requirements.

Acknowledgements

Thanks to Renee Pershinsky for proofreading. Thank you to Mitch Horton, Mark Taisey, Mark Doak, Patrick Palattella, Mike Wheatley in Ferro procurement for providing raw material data. Laboratory work was done by Lou Gazo, Ralph Villoni, Holger Evele, Dana Fick, and Kyla McKinley in the Development Lab. Finally, thanks to Brad Devine in Sales for thinking outside the box regarding bolder raw material substitution ideas.

References (Endnotes)

[1] L. Hall, "Long-Range Availability of Frit Raw Materials," *Proc. PEI Tech Forum* **36**, pp. 100-108 (1974).

[2] E. Alonso and J. Clark, "How Critical are Critical Materials?", *Proc. PEI Tech Forum* **74**, pp. 1-19 (2013).

[3] A. Lynch, "Role of Cobalt Oxide in Porcelain Enamels," *Proc. PEI Tech Forum* **54**, pp. 52-57.

[4] H. Aldersey-Williams, *Periodic Tales: A Cultural History of the Elements, From Arsenic to Zinc*, (Viking: New York, 2011), pp. 305-321.

[5] "Cobalt" http://minerals.usgs.gov/minerals/pubs/commodity/cobalt/myb1-2011-cobal.pdf August 29, 2013.

[6] D. Yearick, L. Smith, and N. Sedalia, "Industry Experiences with No-Cobalt/Low-Cobalt Systems: A Panel Presentation," *Proc. PEI Tech Forum* **42**, pp. 313-315 (1980).

[7] J. Walls, "The Outlook for Cobalt," *Proc. PEI Tech Forum* **44**, pp. 374-5 (1982).

[8] "Cobalt Statistics" http://minerals.usgs.gov/ds/2005/140/ds140-cobal.pdf January 11, 2013.

[9] "Cobalt Mineral Exploration and Supply From 1995 Through 2013"

http://pubs.usgs.gov/sir/2011/5084/pdf/SIR2011-5084_final_012612.pdf September 3, 2013.

[10]"Congo Raises Tax on Copper, Cobalt Concentrates by Two-Thirds" http://www.bloomberg.com/news/2013-07-25/congo-raises-tax-on-copper-cobalt-concentrates-by-two-thirds.html September 9, 2013.

[11] D. Yearick, et al,*op. cit.*, pp. 313-315.

[12]L. Bragina et al., "One-Frit Nickel-Free Antibacterial Vitreous Enamels," *Proc. 22nd International Enameling Congress* (2012).

[13]"Nickel Smelting and Refining http://www.ifc.org/wps/wcm/connect/469da18048855b7f891cdb6a6515bb18/nickel_PPAH.pdf?MOD=AJPERES September 3, 2013.

[14]"Nickel" http://minerals.usgs.gov/minerals/pubs/commodity/nickel/mcs-2013-nicke.pdf September 3, 2013.

[15]"Zirconium and Hafnium" http://minerals.usgs.gov/minerals/pubs/commodity/zirconium/ September 3, 2013.

[16]"Rutile" http://en.wikipedia.org/wiki/Rutile September 4, 2013.

[17]"Anatase" http://en.wikipedia.org/wiki/Anatase September 4, 2013.

[18]R.D. Shannon and A.L. Friedberg, "Titania Opacified Porcelain Enamels," *University of Illinois Bulletin* Vol. 57 No. 44 (Feb., 1960), p.8.

[19]"Titanium Dioxide," *Ceramic Industry* Vol. 159 No. 1 (Jan. 2009), p.105.

[20]M. Horton, "Porcelain Enamel Raw Materials Dynamics," *Proc. PEI Tech Forum* **69**, unpublished, (2007).

[21]"Lithium Use in Batteries" http://pubs.usgs.gov/circ/1371/ September 4, 2013.

[22]S. Fletcher, *Bottled Lightning*, (Hill and Wang: New York, 2011), p.59.

[23]E. Alonso and J. Clark, "How Critical are Critical Materials?", *Proc. PEI Tech Forum* **74**, pp. 1-19 (2013).

[24]L. Hall, *op. cit.*, pp. 100-108.

[25]R. Petrucci, *General Chemistry: Principles and Modern Applications Fifth Edition*, (Macmillian: New York, 1989), p. 895.

[26]S. Feldman et. al., "Next Generation Evolution® Coatings," *Proc. PEI Tech Forum 73,* pp. 77-85 (2012).

Twenty-First Century Cleaning Systems

Ken Kaluzny
Coral Chemical Company

You probably received the same brochure that I received in early April. I was surprised to see my name. I wasn't aware that I was giving a paper this year let alone the title. When I saw my topic I thought "WOW, 21st Century cleaning systems." The brochure stated that I was going to discuss advances in cleaner chemistries and their advantages in porcelain enamel lines. No problem, we all have jobs that show up on our desk when we least expect them. My first question after who signed me up for this gig was "who is using new cleaning chemistry for porcelain enamel pretreatment?" This sounds like space age stuff. The state of the art cleaning chemistry is generally used in highly technical industries for things like semiconductors, computer storage media, or space shuttle circuitry. State of the art technologies are typically expensive. You would probably need to modify or add equipment. Research and development costs generally are reflected in the chemistry cost. I don't want to downplay our industry but porcelain enamel pretreatment isn't rocket science.

I would rather present a different focus. I see the operative words being cleaning systems and view the 21st century as being our current business climate. My presentation will focus on the cleaning system rather than particularly new chemistry. I will discuss some process strategies that address manufacturing concerns that will help you survive and thrive in the 21st Century.

For many of us we are living in a survival mode. Global competition has been affecting our business decisions for some time now. However our current economy, local and global, has given many of us a survival mode mentality. Innovation is essential now more than ever. We need to be innovative with not only our products but with our processes as well.

Successful American manufacturing operations are meeting the challenges of outsourcing and fierce overseas competition via innovation, investment, lean manufacturing, and training. Innovative products, finished goods or manufacturing chemistry, help prevent us from competing solely on price. Process innovation is essential to our ability to compete and maintain a profit.

Environmental issues have driven change in our country as well as in our industry. Whether legitimately created by man or not global warming is a hot topic. It appears that global warming is a sustainable term to the point of begetting new terminology. Did you ever think that someone would be interested in your or their carbon foot print? Marketers weren't too far behind and "Green" is a term that has been great for marketing. I will discuss how becoming "Green" can help you cut operating costs. Simply stated we will look at how we can apply the environmentalists' saying of Reduce, Reuse, and Recycle to your P/E pretreatment.

Whether a trendy marketing approach or not, applying "green" attributes to cleaning operations creates 21st Century Cleaning systems. I will focus on applying the 3-R's to your porcelain pretreatment system: Reduce, Reuse, Recycle.

Before we go green let's talk about what chemical trends are continuing in the 21st century for the enamellers. Ambient cleaners are becoming more common but aren't really a 21st century chemical revelation. Ambient cleaners have been around for a long time. In the 21st century, or particularly the current business climate, ambient cleaners are a hot topic as energy costs are high and sales are typically down. The use of the word ambient is somewhat ambiguous. Ambient temperature in Fargo, ND is going to be different than ambient temperature in Orlando, FL in most any month of the year. Low temperature cleaning would be more accurate and appropriate terminology for the pretreatment process. Some soils just need some heat to become fluid making the cleaning chemistry more effective.

Other continuing trends are driven by environmental health and safety. The elimination of "bad actors" like phosphates and nonylphenol ethoxylates continues at a definite yet uncertain pace. The elimination of bad actors could be the result of waste water discharge regulations or from corporate policy to reduce or eliminate SARA Title III reporting. The elimination of bad actors is also driven by the cost associated with disposal. Phosphates are commonly used in alkaline cleaners and are high on the bad actor list in states such as Minnesota. The trend is continuing to other states as well.

Neutral cleaners are also a recent trend that is driven by environmental health and safety issues. I have formulated and sell neutral cleaners. They can work but they aren't for every cleaning process.

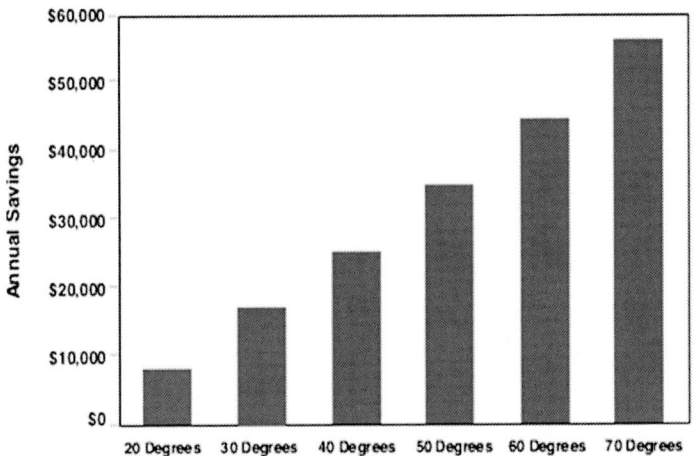

Figure 1. Annual savings as a function of temperature reduction

Figure 1 shows the relationship of energy savings resulting from lowering temperature incrementally 10 degrees. Don't get caught up on the absolute numbers as they relate to a particular set of energy costs, tank size and operating time. If you want to gain a better idea of what you could save on your line, then ask your cleaner vendor. The point that I want to leave you with is that this relationship of temperature and cost is not linear. In other words, dropping your cleaner temperature 10°F produces more savings at 150°F than it does at 120°F. The lower your operating temperature, the lower the savings potential from temperature reduction. I want to caution you that running at 80°F sounds like a huge energy savings if you are operating at 140°F. It is a big savings, but if you start producing rejects, your energy savings will be offset and possibly eliminated. For your system there is a sweet spot for the cleaner temperature in which it will remove soils from your metal without producing a rejected part.

You can apply all of the 3-R's to water. Counter-flowing rinses can reduce water consumption while maintaining quality. Closed loop systems involve multiple rinses incorporating counter-flow rinsing and reverse osmosis filtration in the secondary rinse. This also reduces chemical usage as well. Running at low or ambient temperature will also reduce water usage as evaporative loss is minimized. However in the case of a closed loop system, if you run at low temperatures then you will have to discharge water at some point thus losing the benefit of saving chemistry.
Counter-flow or closed loop systems will reduce chemical usage. I know this for a fact as I have seen it affect sales numbers and I have seen it recorded on a computer log from a controller produced by our next speaker. Low temperature products don't necessarily reduce chemical usage. You should verify and validate your process changes. Rinse Aids can be used to reduce energy costs. Rinse aids reduce surface tension making water drain and subsequently dry quicker. This affords the ability to turn dry-off ovens down and reduce energy consumption.

In conclusion, ambient cleaning is not new. However the current business climate is driven by economical and ecological factors. Applying green principles can lower your operating costs to help you survive and/or thrive in today's business climate.

Cleaning and Metal Preparation for Porcelain Enameling

John O'Connor
Calvary Industries

In today's manufacturing, lean is a driving force to help improve quality while increasing production rates. This paper will discuss advances in alkaline cleaning chemistries that allow companies to bypass mechanical and or chemical steps.

The types of oxides that need to be removed are mill scale, laser scale, plasma scale, and weld scale. Cleaning prior to porcelain enameling (and other finishing processes) should consider both organic and inorganic soils. Alkaline cleaner technology is not just focusing on oils and lubricants but rather all contaminants on the surface that need to be removed to ensure proper surface prep for enameling. Oxides from welding can cause parts to be difficult to finish. This forces extra labor either by mechanical or acidic chemical processes.

Speedy removal of organic soils exposes inorganic contaminants on the substrate. Targeted organic soils include:

- Stearates and fatty acid soap drawing compounds
- Mill oils and heavy oil drawing compounds
- Oil/Talc lubricants
- Varnished/partially carbonized hydrocarbons

Detergents and surface active agents are formulated to quickly penetrate and disperse soils/oils and flush them free of the surface.

Once the organics are out of the way, removing oxides and carbon is the key. Selective chelation is able to remove some oxides and impurities from the surface, exposing a uniform substrate. This will not remove the glass from welding or laser oxide. It is a similar mechanism to passivation, but an alkaline operation. Using stereochemistry of soft chelators (not EDTA or NTA) allows the product to be waste treated easily. Figure 1 shows photos of weld scale removal, and Figure 2 shows photos of braze scale removal.

Before Cleaning   After Cleaning

Figure 1. Weld scale removal

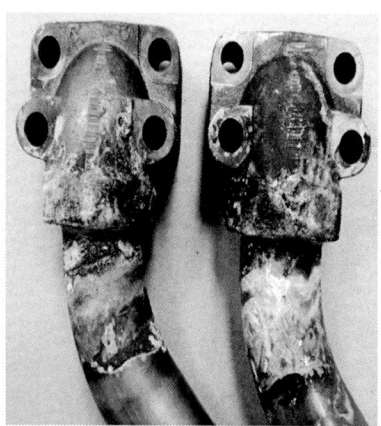 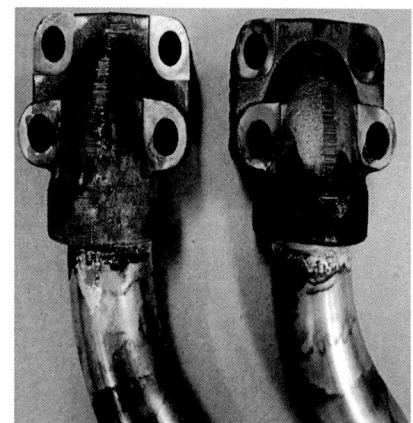

Before Cleaning   After Cleaning

Figure 2. Braze scale removal

Oxides and organics removed can build up in the bath solution and tie up cleaning ingredients. It is important to monitor parameters of the chemical bath to maintain effective cleaning. Figure 3 shows an example. It is important to keep the ratio of total alkalinity and free alkalinity (the materials that can still clean) constant to maximize the bath life.

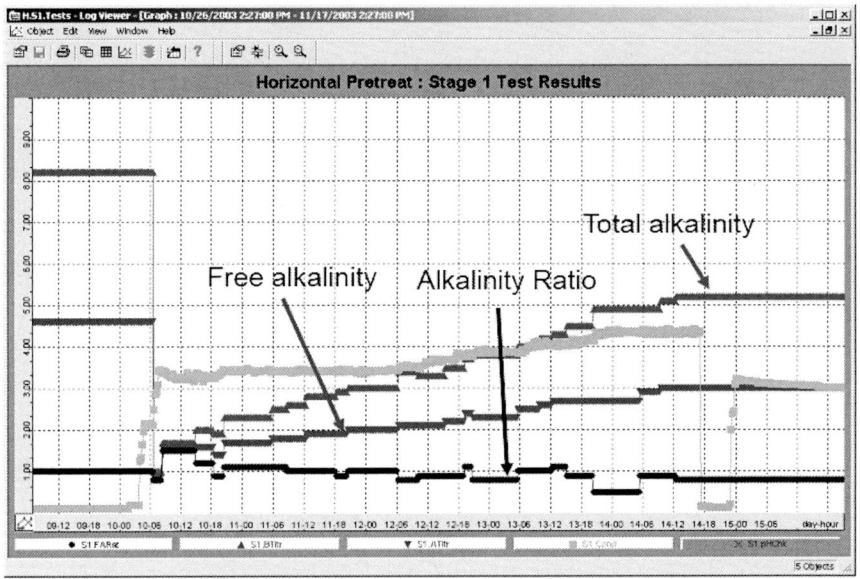

Figure 3. Pretreatment soil loading

In porcelain enameling, it is thus possible to go to one step for cleaning of welded wire grills. One step of alkaline cleaning takes the place of abrasion media blasting followed by alkaline cleaning.

The impact of the total process improvement is better total cleanliness for both oily soils and rust. This then increases first pass yield on coatings. Offline or manual processing is reduced, and acid pickles are eliminated. A high soil load tolerance (both organic and inorganic) allows for longer dump cycles. The bath will hold 8-12 times its concentration in soil.

Washer Fundamentals for Porcelain Enamel

Jeff Studnicka
Americo Chemical Products, Inc.

Understanding washer costs is required to justify improvements and modifications. Washer operating costs include hard costs such as natural gas, water, electricity, and chemicals.

Part 1 – Hard Cost Reductions

To reduce natural gas costs, measure the gas usage through a gas meter at each input to the process. With lower temperature cleaning, understand your soil inputs. Many soils can be cleaned at lower temperatures approaching ambient. Change your soil inputs to help reduce temperature. Design the washer system to retain the heated solution. Backflow semi-heated rinse to the cleaner. Insulate the stage and reclaim unused heat. Focus on energy and install a gas meter to measure gas usage per unit of measure. Install backflow piping to the cleaner stage through a halo. De-scale the cleaner stage to prevent scale formation on the burner tube. Only 1/8" of scale can reduce efficiency by 28%. Better understand the burner control operation to optimize gas usage.

To reduce water usage, measure water usage through flow meters for each input to the process. Re-use water by:

- Having counter flow rinse stages
- Back flowing rinse water to the cleaner bath
- Controlling the conductivity/total dissolved solids (TDS) so water is not being wasted
- Designing the system with fresh water halos to have the cleanest water possible contacting the parts

There are three modifications that can be made to the washer to reduce water usage. First, add piping to backflow rinses. Second, measure rinse water with an automatic or manual conductivity meter. Third, add piping to spray overflow water on the parts and not pour into the contaminated rinse bath. Figure 1 shows a schematic of a washer with counter flows and a halo for efficient water usage.

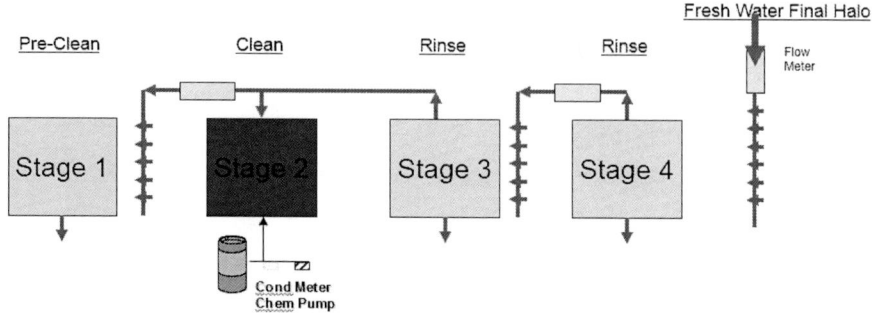

Figure 1. Cleaner system with efficient water usage

To reduce electrical costs, use variable frequency drives on washer pumps. Automatically turn stages off when they are not being used.

To reduce chemical costs:

- Reduce concentration
- Reduce carry-out on parts
- Design drain zones to minimize carry-out
- Mist parts leaving the cleaner stage to drain cleaner off parts exiting the stage
- Clean parts in pre-clean stage

The make-up water for the cleaner stage should be from the following rinse stage. Maintain nozzles to prevent cross-contamination. Add automated process controls.

When modifying the washer design to reduce chemical costs, always look at the hanging procedures to minimize solution carry-out. Change drain zones where necessary. Use a small misting halo at the end of the cleaner bath, and don't overflow the stage. Pre-clean parts with overflow rinse water. Add piping to backflow to your cleaner stage based on level control. Add good controllers to improve process control. Remove oil from the cleaner bath through filtration. This makes the cleaner more effective, extends bath life with more improving cleaning over the entire bath life, and reduces cleanout costs by extending the bath life.

A case study was done for a 5500 gallon alkaline cleaner bath for a dual line system with the first line running 12 fpm for 24 hours/day and the second line running at 6 fpm for 8 hours/day. This customer had an oil coalescer on their cleaner bath for years. They tried a different filtration technology that did not remove the oil effectively. Without removing the oil, the total alkalinity increased much more rapidly over the life of the bath thus reducing the cleaning effectiveness of the bath and increasing the chemical usage. The oil coalescer was put back online and immediately 55 gals of oil were removed from the bath. The total alkalinity was lowered and usage reduced. The oil coalescer extended the bath life approximately 700 - 1000 hours of run time equating into reduced PM costs. 25 % less chemical was used over the life of the bath.

In summary the final results were:

- Bath life with good oil removal: 2500 – 2700 hours
- Bath life without oil removal: 1500 – 1800 hours
- Payback was less than 6 months on the oil coalescer

Part 2 – Soft Cost Reductions

Washer soft costs/inputs to target for savings are line density, process control of system parameters, part presentation, and preventa-

tive maintenance. With line density, clean parts and do not space them. Hang parts as effectively as possible, and apply continuous improvement to the hanging patterns. Process control of system parameters uses automation to maintain tighter control ranges.
With part presentation to spray patterns, allow the mechanical action of the spray patterns to be as effective as possible. Hang parts to minimize swinging and higher pressures.
Design the process so fixtures, racks, and hooks are as effective as possible. Conduct ongoing improvement with new parts and smaller lot sizes; apply the principles of Lean manufacturing. For process control of system parameters, good automation will reduce chemical usage about 10 – 15%.

Summary

There are many inputs to the washer process that are often overlooked. Most modifications to the washer process can be justified with relatively quick payback. Most modifications are not expensive and/or time consuming. Your chemical supplier can help you with these improvements.

Importance of Cleaning and Rinsing Prior to Enameling

Suresh Patel
Chemetall

Any coating process is only as successful as its base metal preparation. Consistently producing a cleaned surface is very important in the enameling process. Poor cleaning hurts subsequent stages and causes poor adhesion. It increases rework costs and warranty claims. It causes process delays and results in dissatisfied customers. Ultimately, it impacts the bottom-line. Good cleaning is a solid foundations on which to build the rest of a coating process.

Outline

- Why Clean?
- Cleaning Fundamentals
- Cleaning Methods
- Cleaning Process
- Cleaning Selection
  - Substrate
  - Soil
  - Cleaning Selection Considerations
  - Cleaning Mechanics
- Process Equipment
- Rinsing
- Cleaning Test Methods
- Maintenance
- Troubleshooting
- Safety

Why Clean?

Parts are cleaned for two different end results:

1. Prior to conversion coating and enameling (coating)

2. Between machining steps and prior to assembly (in-process cleaning)

The purpose is to remove soils that are collected in previous operations from the substrate surfaces and prepare them for subsequent operations such as enameling or coating. Poor cleaning and rinsing are one of the major causes of painted/coated part defects.

Cleaning Fundamentals

Cleaning metals involves not only the selection of the type(s) of cleaners, but also the proper cleaning cycle and process equipment. Having a solid process, which meets or exceeds expectations, must be all encompassing to address soils, metals, water quality, process control and maintenance of the system.

The best way to begin the cleaning process is with a series of questions designed to promote both specifics and generalities that have an impact on the process.

Fact-Finding Questionnaire:

- ❖ What base metals are cleaned?
- ❖ What soils are on the incoming parts?
- ❖ What soils are applied to the metal in-house?
- ❖ What is the production flow of the products?
- ❖ What production assemblies are premanufactured and stored?
- ❖ Do they corrode in storage?
- ❖ Do the soils age or become more difficult to remove later on?
- ❖ Is the cleaning process capable of removing all soils e.g. mill scale?
- ❖ What are the physical size limitations of your products?
- ❖ During welding and fabricating, are soils entrapped or sandwiched between metals?
- ❖ Do you preclean prior to welding? If not, how much carbonaceous residue is left on or near weldments? Is oil entrapped in

these areas?
- ❖ What is the quality of the water to be used in the cleaning operation? Conductivity? Hardness? Chlorides and sulfates?
- ❖ Process mechanics?
- ❖ And others...

Cleaning Methods

The three types of cleaning are mechanical, solvent, and aqueous. Mechanical uses metal impingement with sand blasting, steel shot blasting, etc. Solvent cleaning is wipe cleaning or flow over sink-on-a-drum. The focus for enameling is aqueous cleaning over the whole pH range from acidic to neutral to alkaline with either single or multi-stage washers with spray and/or immersion washing.

The advantages of mechanical cleaning are reclaim and reuse lowers cost of use for media. It is a single step process that removes most inorganic contaminants. Impingement roughs up metal surface, which is good for paint adhesion. On the other hand, the disadvantages are it is not applicable for thorough removing of organics. Imbedded media and dust can interfere with subsequent coatings. It may damage or change dimensions of critical parts, and it provides no under paint corrosion protection.

The advantages of solvent cleaning are (1) excellent removal of organic contaminants, (2) can be used cold or hot, and (3) does not require water rinsing to remove process chemistry. The disadvantages are the wipe or immersion processes can redeposit soils and there is no ability to remove inorganic contaminants. The solvents are flammable, which creates worker exposure issues. The process provides no increase in either paint adhesion or corrosion resistance and is heavily regulated.

Aqueous cleaning has clear environmental advantages over solvent cleaning for no VOCs, no flammability, etc. Numerous washer designs are available to match application need (e.g., spray, immersion). It can be matched to the next step in process such as phosphating, etc. Soils can be separated from solution via separation/filtration techniques. On the other hand, the disadvantages are the cost of chemical, water, energy, and equipment as well as the maintenance cost of the equipment (nozzles, clean-outs, etc.). It also requires solution control and testing.

Cleaning Process

The cleaning process is selected from the following options:
- Continuous and Batch
- Multi-stage processes
- Spray/continuous

The focus of this article will be spray/continuous. An example is in Figure 1.

Figure 1. Modular belt conveyor washer

Figure 2 shows a typical five stage spray washer schematic. Cascades and halos can cut water use in half.

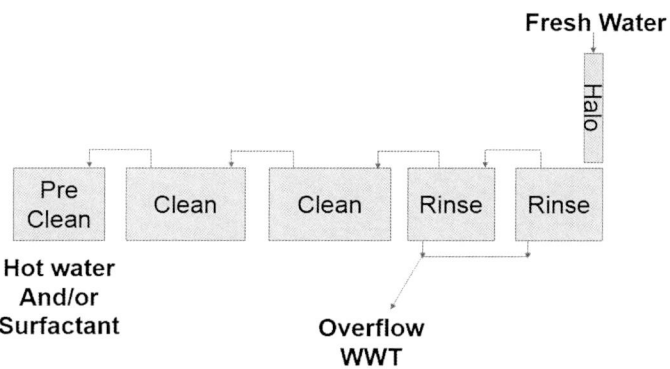

Figure 2. Typical cleaning process

Cleaner Selection

Cleaner selection is very important. Considerations include the substrate, soils, cleaning mechanics, process equipment, water quality, and environmental and disposal concerns, such as NPE-free surfactants or phosphate-free cleaners.

With enameling, steel is the most common substrate coated. The steel used is cold-rolled, hot-rolled, or enameling grade. Cast iron is the second most common substrate followed by aluminum. Rarely, copper or other metals are coated.

Soils are either organic or inorganic contaminants. Organics include oils, coolants, waxes, greases, hydraulic fluids, buffing compounds and mold release agents. Inorganics include metal oxides, rust, laser scale, water stains, mill scale, sanding fines and shop dust and dirt. More difficult to remove contaminants include silicones, heavy high temperature greases, surface defects, burnt on soils, old/polymerized soils and paraffinic soils.

Factors affecting organic soils are the soil's age, any heat exposure, or extreme pressure (EP) agents like chlorinated, sulfonated esters. With ageing, soluble oil and semi-synthetic fluids dry out and invert. Some soils polymerize over time. Exposure to heat can come from metal working operations such as welding, annealing, or heat treating.

There are several questions to answer when specifying the cleaner. The process is spray or immersion, but should the cleaner be acid, alkaline or neutral? Acid cleaners are used to attack problems like oxides from laser cutting and mill scale. Neutral cleaners are typically used when substrate soil is very limited. Alkaline cleaners do the bulk of the work when surface contamination is organic in nature. Lowering the operating temperature can save some significant energy dollars. Should the cleaner be powder or liquid? Oil splitting or emulsifying? What are the amount and types of oils to be removed and how to remove them? What types of oil removal equipment should be used and should it be designed for floating/skimming, ultrafiltration, etc.? Etching or non-etching? Galvanized and aluminum substrates can be severely etched by some cleaning products. Be mindful of what you're trying to accomplish when selecting a cleaner. Phosphated or phosphate free? Certain areas of the country have strict phosphate discharge limits for wastewater. Keep in mind the type of substrate and nature of the surface contaminants (oil, grease, dirt, lubes, etc.) may necessitate using phosphates. Other factors are workers safety, environmental concerns, waste water treatment costs, and used costs.

New trends in cleaners are phosphorous-free--both elemental phosphorous and phosphate (PO_4)-free. Some examples of watershed areas requiring less than 1-25 mg/L phosphorous are:

- ❖ Areas of Minnesota
- ❖ Areas of Wisconsin
- ❖ Chicago
- ❖ Areas of Canada, Toronto, Montreal for example
- ❖ Chesapeake Bay, Virginia
- ❖ Spokane River, Washington

- Great Lakes, New York, Michigan, etc
- Hudson River, New York
- Chattahoochee River, Georgia
- Others

Another trend is NonylPhenol Ethoxylate (NPE)-Free. NPE is banned in Europe and Canada, and the US EPA intends to initiate action to restrict NPE use. NPEs have many uses, but they are primarily used as surfactants in cleaning chemical formulations, as wetting agents and as dispersants or emulsifiers in some pesticide formulations. However, NPE and NonylPhenol (NP) are teratogens and are bad for the environment, bad for wildlife and bad for people. A third trend is low-temperature cleaners.

Process Equipment

Key factors affecting cleaner performance can be summed up with "T.A.C.T.":

- Contact **T**ime
- Physical **A**ction
  - Spray Pressure / Coverage
  - Agitation of immersion tanks
  - Ultrasonic
  - Electrolytic cleaning
  - Brushes/Wiping
- Cleaner **C**oncentration, Type
- Cleaner Solution **T**emperature

Other factors affecting cleaner performance are water quality (the "universal solvent"), pH, and contamination.

T.A.C.T. and other factors are the problem solvers and keys to optimum cleaning results. Variance of one factor will often require the adjustment of one or more of the other factors.

The bath needs to be automatically controlled. Chemical reaction and drag-out cause bath conductivity to decrease. A conductivity sensor will detect the decrease. Chemical will then be pumped at an assigned feed rate till pre-set level is reached. This is especially good for lines with variable throughput of metal surface area.

Alternately, time feed of chemical from a feed pump is especially good for lines with constant throughput of metal surface area. To check the feed pump rate, direct feed pump output into a graduated cylinder. Measure the amount, measure the ratio, and adjust as needed.

Auxiliary equipment is used for oil/soil removal. Oil removal is with oil skimmers to remove free-floating oils or with ultra filters to screen out emulsified oils. The three types of skimmers are disk, belt, or rope. Soil removal is with filters (bag, cartridge, or filter press) or centrifuges. Filters are used for removal of particulate soils typically at higher volume applications, and filter media can be automatically replaced. Bag and cartridge filters are generally used for removal of particulate soils with side stream or full flow. Centrifugal separators like cyclones or centrifuges utilize inertia to separate soil particles from solution.
The benefits of oil/soil removal are extended bath life, increased cleaner efficiency, reduced cleaner usage, reduced maintenance costs, and improved overall part cleanliness/quality.

Rinsing

If "clean" means that all unwanted soils have been removed in the cleaning step, then the downstream step of rinsing is necessary to achieve that cleanliness. The only way to produce perfectly cleaned parts is to rinse them with good quality water.

Rinsing stops the chemical reaction from the previous stage, removes chemicals from the previous stage, and prevents contamination of the subsequent stage. If rinsing is poor, it doesn't matter how good the rest of the process is. Poor rinsing leads to:

- Cross-contamination of process chemicals
- Visually objectionable parts
- Streaks
- Spots
- Field failure of finished parts
- Blisters
- Delamination
- Corrosion

Performance factors affecting rinsing are contamination (chlorides, sulfates), hardness, acidity and alkalinity), temperature, contact time, and solution movement through pressure or agitation. Other considerations with rinsing are counterflow, misting after the chemical stage, a fresh water riser after the rinse stage, and the conductivity/total dissolved solids (TDS) of the drip water. Hard water can cause scale, can react with soaps creating sludge that clogs nozzles, has a higher surface tension and less ability to sheet, is less corrosive, and is less prone to foam. Soft water has a low tendency to scale, had lower surface tension with more ability to sheet, is more corrosive, more prone to foam, and has a higher sodium content. Table 1 compares rinse water purified as deionized (DI) water to purification with reverse osmosis (RO).

Deionized Water (DI)
Hard water salts removed by resin
Ca and Mg replaced by H
Cl and SO_4 replaced by OH
TDS typically < 7 ppm
Conductivity typically < 10 mS/cm

Reverse Osmosis (RO)
Removes most organic and many inorganic molecules by membrane separation at high pressure
TDS typically 7 - 35 ppm
Conductivity typically 10 - 50 mS/cm
Hard water salts (Ca) often first removed by water softener

Table 1. Comparison of deionized (DI) and reverse osmosis (RO) for purifying rinse water

Automation with rinsing uses digital and analog rinse tank controllers. Conductivity is measured, and the controller operates a solenoid valve.

Drying methods are air evaporation, compressed air blow off, air knife, drying in an oven, infrared lamp banks, or a cloth wipe. The cleaner chemistry can also affect drying characteristics. Cleaners with low surface tension tend to have reduced drag-out and subsequently dry faster.

Cleaning Test Methods

Four common methods to measure the surface cleanliness are:

- ❖ Wipe test
- ❖ Water break
- ❖ Gravimetric
- ❖ Tape test

Other methods are visual, Coulometric surface carbon, fluorescence, radiotracer, scanning electron microscopy (SEM), energy dispersive X-ray analysis (EDXA), or Fourier Transform Infrared (FTIR) spectroscopy.

Maintenance

Cleaner items that require regular routine maintenance are screens, filters, nozzles, the descale tank, heat exchangers, pumps, exhaust, skimmers, conveyor, etc. Always keep good records of maintenance and process parameters.

Troubleshooting

When troubleshooting, define the problem and ask what changed? Locate the source of the problem. Chemical or mechanical? Test one variable at a time. Implement change, and verify.

Poor cleaning, corrosion/rust, streaked/spotted parts, or foaming can all lead to trouble. Learn to spot them and methodically troubleshoot one variable at a time.

Safety

The MSDS (Material Safety Data Sheet) lists hazardous ingredients, defines hazards, recommends Personal Protective Equipment (PPE), and recommends accident remediation. MSDS files need to be kept it in a convenient location.

Summary

The fundamentals, materials, and equipment of the cleaning process were reviewed. New trends in phosphorous and NPE-free cleaners were highlighted.

Importance of Cleaning and Rinsing Prior to Enameling

Anyone can purchase and use an aqueous cleaning system which will remove soils from the parts.

The "Trick" to continually producing clean parts requires a solid process and robust rinsing.

Cleaning and rinsing are the most critical steps in any coating process.

Rack Rotation for Process-to-Furnace Conveyor Transfer

Richard A. Dooley
Mighty Hook, Inc.

In-plane alignment in the corona zone and smooth rotation at the transfer station are both necessary for a double-sided electrostatic porcelain powder spray process line. This paper discusses some recent developments of fixture design.

Introduction

Our quest for conveyor tooling projects in the more demanding end of the spectrum has led to several advances in the design of rotators and indexers. It is a common understanding among the practitioners of both that electrostatic porcelain powder application is at least an order of magnitude more difficult than its organic powder counterpart. Relative reluctance to accept a charge and the higher specific gravity of the material conspire to form a tightrope that production operators must walk every working day of their careers. Handling in the manual transfer between processing and furnace conveyors of powder coated is a particularly delicate spot. Just one tap can lead to one little avalanche that sends the part to rework. Attempts have been made, at a sacrifice in versatility, to link processing and firing by a single conveyor. Another opportunity is to effectively double processing line capacity by mounting parts on both sides of the racks. This has been a long-standing aspiration - and one that is crucially dependent on a smooth automatic rotation of the rack at the transfer station, to enable unloading of the second side.

Designers of high speed, cam-driven machine elements have long used a simple time versus displacement relationship termed a *Cycloid* to control actuation because it results in low noise, vibration, and wear. A cycloid is very simple to visualize; it is the path of a point on the circumference of a circle as it rolls along a planar surface (Figure 1). With velocity plotted on the x-axis and the circle rolling at a constant speed, as the point "unsticks" the travel path is nearly vertical with only a tiny x-axis component. At the 180° rotational position, the point is moving at twice the travel velocity of the circle. The opposite occurs during the second 180° - the point again moves with an imperceptible x-axis component just prior to contact.

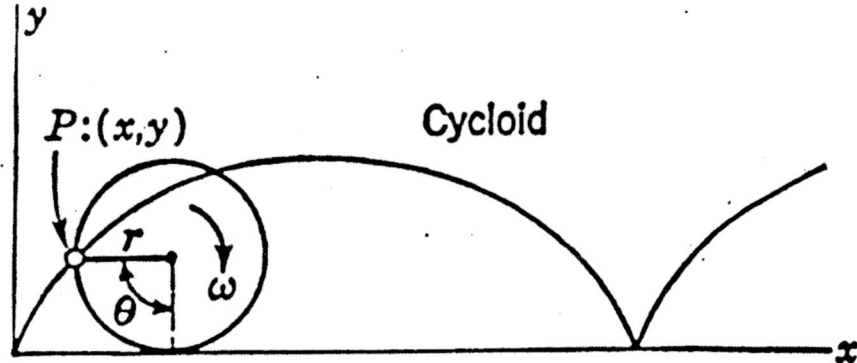

Figure 1. Generation of Cycloid Curve

Velocity and acceleration versus time relationships through a 360° circle travel are shown in Figure 2. Note that there are no abrupt changes in the acceleration curve. Displacement versus time relationship is also shown as curve AB. In a previous life, the author had good success using cycloidal techniques in the design of control cams for high speed hydraulic servo-powered painting robots.

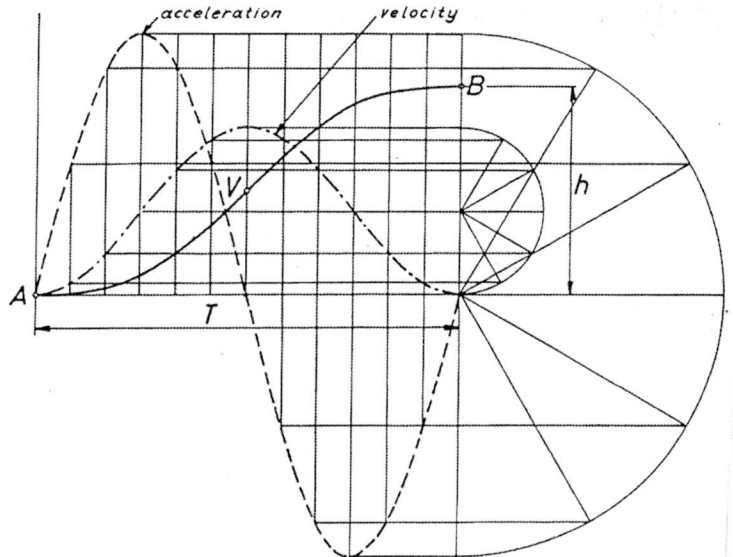

Figure 2. Cycloidal Displacement, Velocity, and Acceleration versus Time

Application to Rotator System

Recently we were invited to develop a rotator system for the transfer station of a new electrostatic powder processing line. Space was at a premium and line speed was high at 24 feet per minute. No simple star wheel or sprocket-driven rotator would have had a chance. We decided to combine our proven braked washer and pin detent with a modified torpedo drive and use the cycloidal technique to contour the drive tracks. The results are shown in Figures 3, 4, 5, and 6.

Figure 3 shows the rotator. Conveyor travel is left-to-right. For more accurate tracking and minimum envelope height a double H-Attachment mount was used; rigid on the front and flexible fore-and-aft on the rear. Torpedoes are mounted in the standard ar-

Figure 3. Cycloidal-Driven Torpedo Rotator

Figure 4. Transfer Station Actuator Track Assembly, in Operating Position

Figure 5. Loading Station Actuator Track Assembly, in Retracted Position

Figure 6. Up-line View of Actuator Track Assembly

rangement (top parallel and bottom lateral to the conveyor) and are radiused on their leading contact surfaces to provide a more even drive torque. Instead of a solid connection, detent pins are weld-assembled to a transverse pin through a clearance hole in the axle shaft. This provides forgiveness for small angular and lateral position uncertainties in the mounting of the detent washer. Although it doesn't show clearly, the washer is initially welded to a sleeve which rotates freely in the central tube of the frame. This permits the final alignment of the rack mounting pin to the rotator frame to be accurately done in a fixture, with the visible tack welds then applied after a true 90° orientation is established.

The transfer station actuator track assembly is shown in Figure 4. At the top, over-center mechanisms controlled from the handles in the foreground enable instant retraction of the tracks, to simply disengage them or to free a stuck rotator (Figure 5 - this is the hang-on area actuator track assembly). The reason for splitting them is a little more subtle. With the rack spacing on the conveyor at 40" and a total track length of 48", it would be necessary to hand-align one rotator to engage the entire track "on the fly". As it is, there is plenty of time to bring the first track down between racks, and then the second track in turn as the previous rack/rotator clears it.
An up-line view from the actuator track exit shows the *Delrin™* plastic tracks to good advantage in Figure 6. Curvature of the driving surfaces which contact the torpedoes is apparent. The bottom pair of straight tracks maintains the bottom end of the rotator at ±.060" from the conveyor centerline throughout the transit. Vertical tracks in the foreground lift under the top torpedo to provide smooth re-engagement of the rotator detent.

Operation of the Rotator System

After the inevitable tuning and tweaking, operation of the rotator system at full line speed is very smooth. Although not shown, some of the workpieces have a hole in their top flange, through which a single pin secures them to the rack. Our criterion for success was that the parts could not "rattle" on the rack at any point during the transit through the actuator tracks. For a short time prior to installation of the tracks, the racks were being rotated manually. Seeing how the tracks were intended to work, we strongly suspect that the production transfer operators themselves brought them to their final standard of tuning – during a recent visit to the plant, MH people were not permitted to touch them!

Rack Rotation for Process-to-Furnace Conveyor Transfer

Track Design Procedure and Calculations:

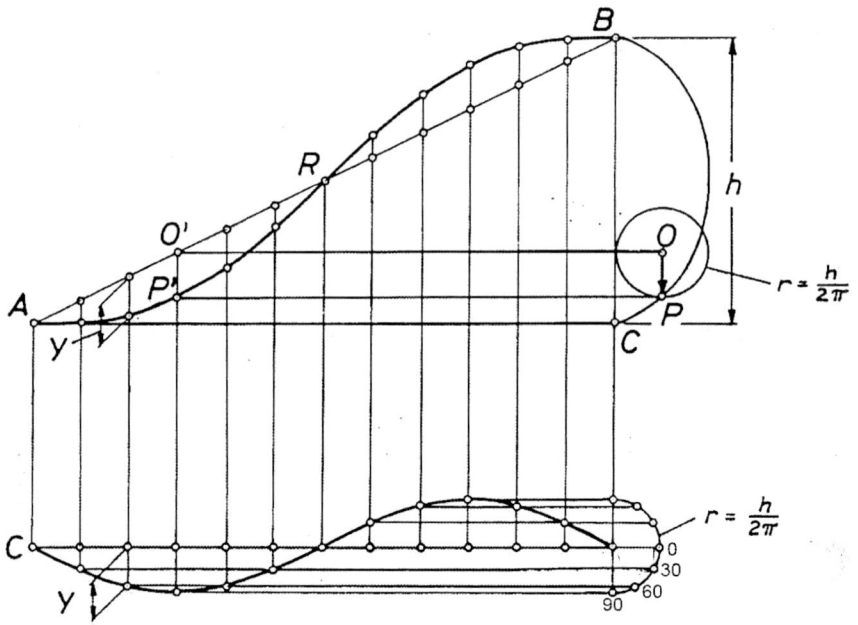

Figure 7a and 7b. Derivation of Cycloidal Displacement Curve

Geometric development of the cycloidal displacement Curve AB in Figure 2 is shown in isolated form in Figure 7a. The straight line which connects these two points represents the constant speed of the generating circle axle, Point O. Point P is a point on the circumference of the circle which rolls on the straight line BC. The Radius OP of the circle is made equal to $h/2\pi$ so the circumference of the circle equals the distance BC. The circle begins to roll upwards when P is at C. When the center of the circle is at the position shown, Point P has moved to its present position. A horizontal line is drawn from O to O', which is on Line AB, and a vertical line is drawn from O' to intersect the horizontal line through P; the point of the intersection is P' which is a point on the displacement curve.

As shown in Figure 7b, cycloidal motion can also be considered to be composed of a straight line AB on which is superimposed a sine wave, the amplitude of which is h/2π; this amplitude being perpendicular to the baseline AC. Skewing AC vertically upward from Point A to Point C and maintaining the ordinates in a vertical orientation will show the similitude of the two figures.

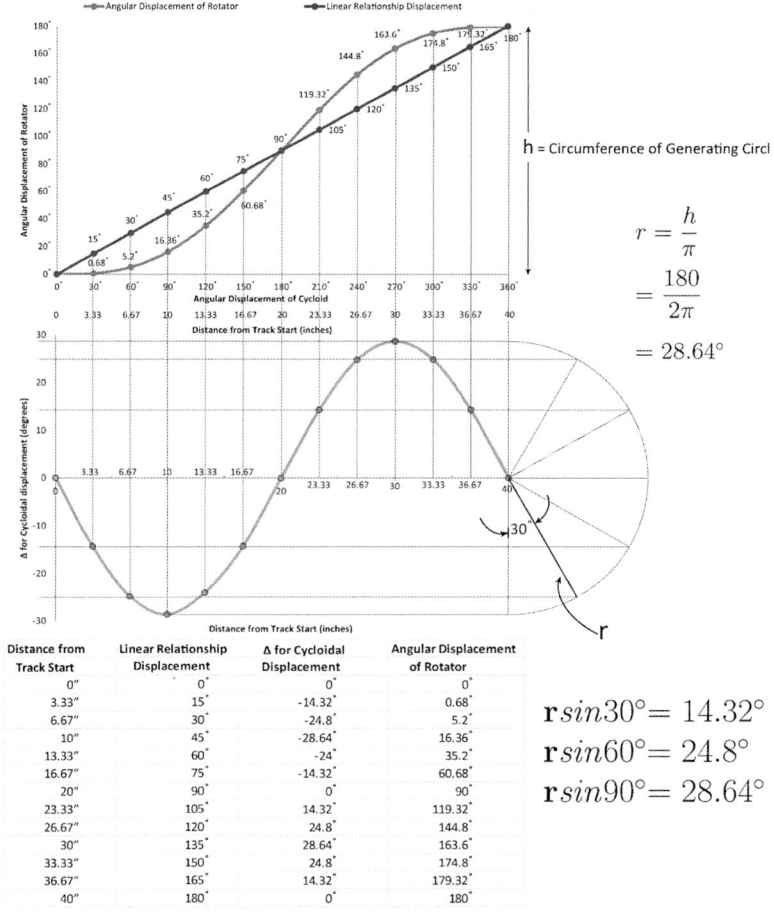

Figure 8. Rotation versus Linear Displacement Graph & Chart. Graphs correspond to Figures 7a & 7b with Vertical Scales Expanded for Clarity. Numerical Values are for Subject Rotator System.

To illustrate the application to rotator design, a worked example will be given, using the actual design parameters of this project. This begins with a chart and a graph which substitute actual numerical values for the previous symbols (Figure 8). A top view is then prepared, preferably at full-scale, showing the axle positions of both top and bottom torpedoes at their proper linear displacements from the initial zero-degree/zero-displacement point (Figure 9).

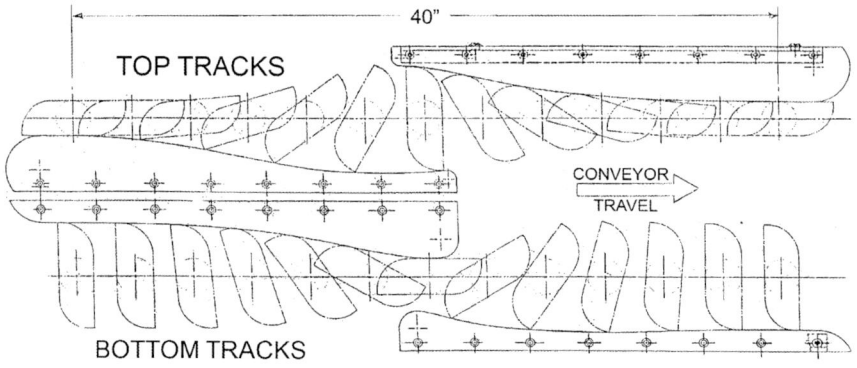

Figure 9. Plotting of Actuator Track Control Surfaces

From here the respective angular displacements are added and the top views of the torpedoes in each position are drawn. The final step is to contour the inner drive surfaces of the tracks to match the outside surfaces of the torpedoes at their successive locations.

Conclusions

This article has described an improved approach, cycloidal displacement, for driving powered rotators at high conveyor speeds. A successful case study has been presented, and a numerical and graphical technique to enable easy application in similar situations has been suggested. Other possibilities for use certainly exist: one being a controlled spin-up for sprocket rotation drives in the corona zones of booths coating radially symmetrical parts.

References
Jensen, Preben, "Cam Design and Manufacture"; The Industrial Press, New York, NY; 1965.

Understand and Interpreting Temperature Profiles

Brian Rozdilsky
KMI Systems Inc

Temperature Profiles

An enamel shop interested in good process control purchases and gets trained on a Datapaq. They run their first furnace profile, and then what?

The first step is to analyze the graph. A reasonably flat curve has advantages:

- It is simple to confirm adequate cure based on time at temperature without having to perform a % cure analysis
- Elimination of hot spots
- Elimination of cold spots

What you don't want to see is in Figure 1.

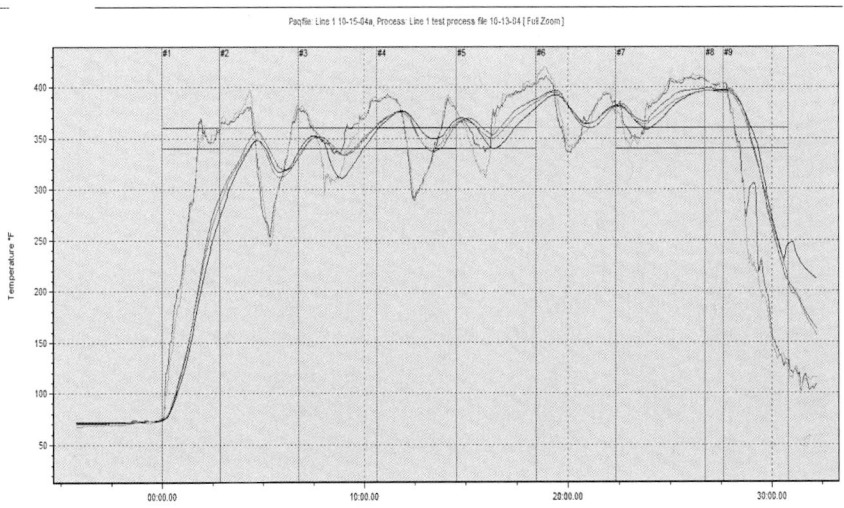

Figure 1. Undesirable furnace profile

Unfortunately, the issue then gets fixed the wrong way. The operator makes changes to the oven and does not record original settings. The temperature is turned up, burners are adjusted, and/or the conveyor is slowed down. Sometimes it helps, sometimes it get worse. This happens because the operator typically makes assumptions about the time when the Datapaq enters the oven.

The correct way to fix the issue is to understand factors that affect temperature in the furnace or oven such as:

- Inadequate air flow
- Misdirected air flow
- Unwanted infiltration air
- Poor exhaust
- Out of tune burners

Of course, it is important to know where the parts are as they travel through the furnace.

The first step is proper probe placement. An example is shown in Figure 2.

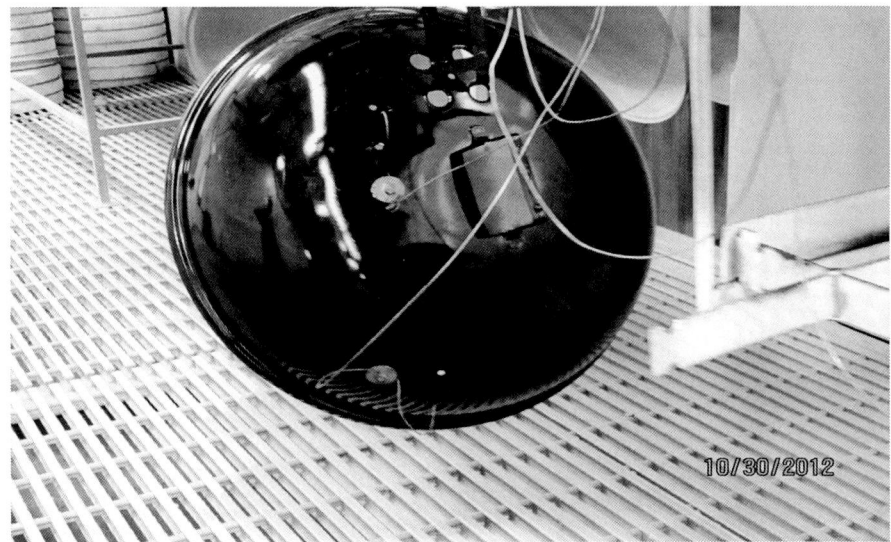

Figure 2. Furnace profile probe placement on a BBQ grill lid

All ovens draw at least some make up air in through the oven part openings whether the oven is elevated or floor mounted. However, air flow problems result in cold spots and the peaks and valleys on Figure 1. When running a profile, note exact time when the Datapaq is started and then the exact time the Datapaq enters the oven. The air probe will spike when the Datapaq enters the oven. Now it will be possible to accurately map out temperature along the conveyor path. This works for both continuous and indexing ovens. Record damper positions. Analyze the overlay that is shown in Figure 3. If cold air is drawn into the oven through conveyor openings, recirculation ductwork needs adjustment. Look for temperature stratification from low circulation and low air velocity or due to improperly balanced burners. Temperature changes could also be due to incorrect set points.

Understand and Interpreting Temperature Profiles

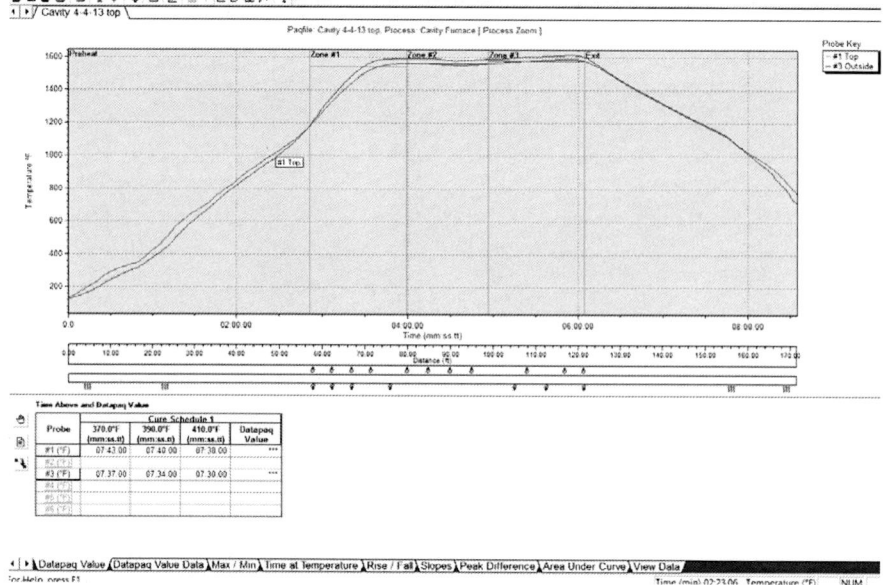

Figure 3. Furnace profile with overlay

Timing when the probe enters the furnace allows understanding of where problems are in the furnace. For example, Figure 4 shows the schematic of the furnace profiled in Figure 3.

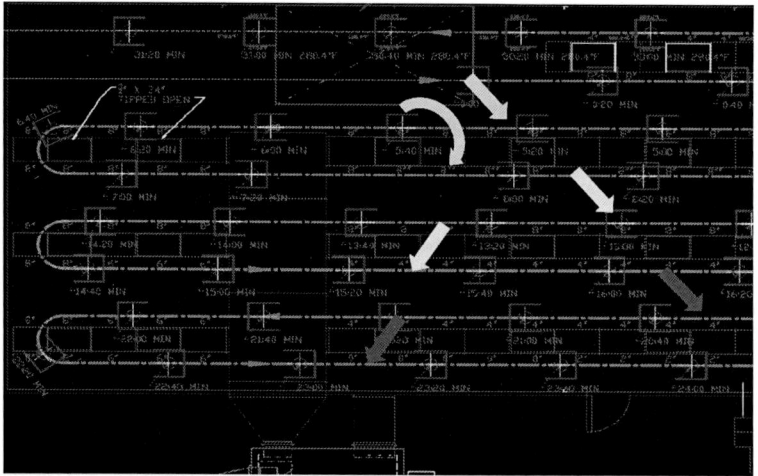

Figure 4. Furnace schematic

Figure 5 shows a desirable profile after repairs were made to the air flow problem causing cold spots.

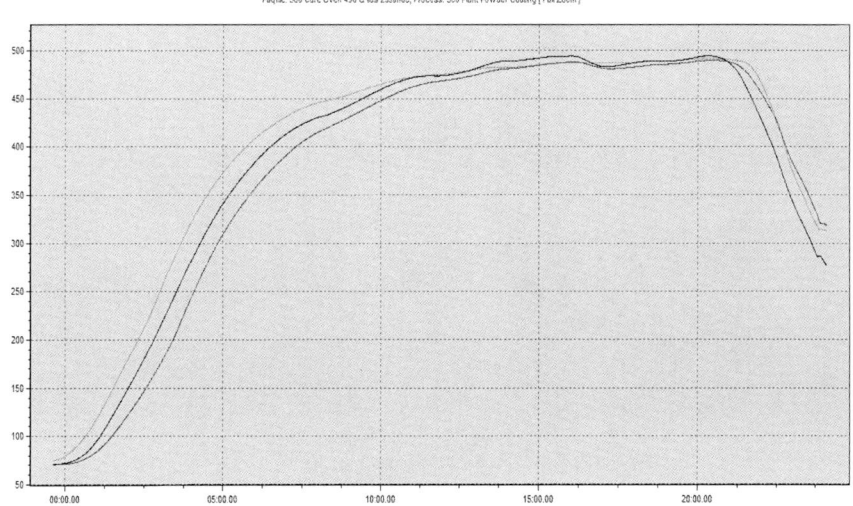

Figure 5. Desirable furnace profile

Case Study

An enameller was firing large agricultural parts in an indexing oven with bottom entry. Before the fix, parts were not adequately curing, and part temperature varied as much as 100°F side to side. A cross-section schematic of the furnace is shown in Figure 6.

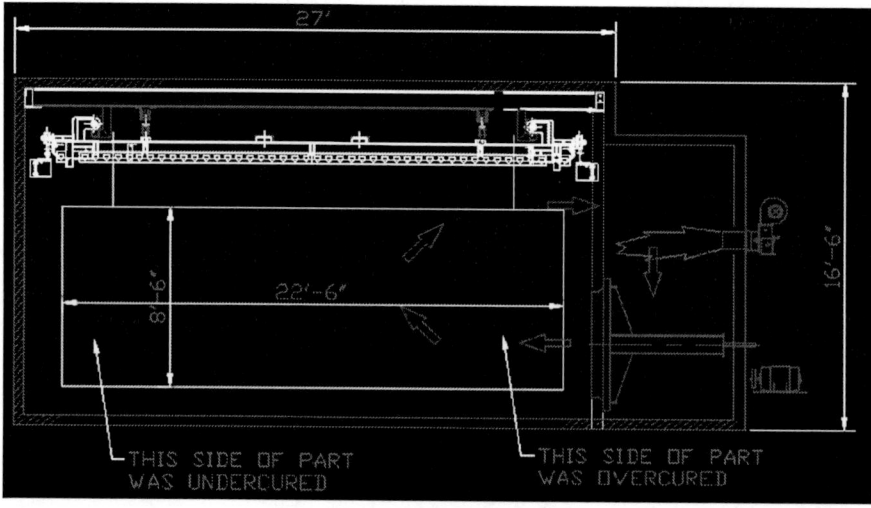

Figure 6. Case study furnace before fix

After repairs, the distribution of circulation air was redesigned, and the temperature was uniform side to side. A schematic of the modified furnace showing the air flow changes to make the temperature uniform is in Figure 7.

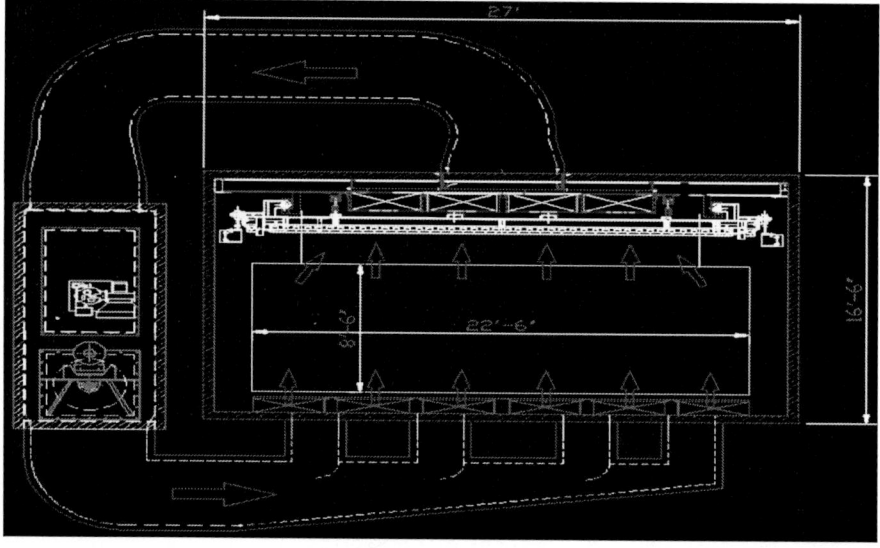

Figure 7. Case study furnace after fix

The furnace profile before the air flow changes is in Figure 8. Note the spikes and uneven temperature.

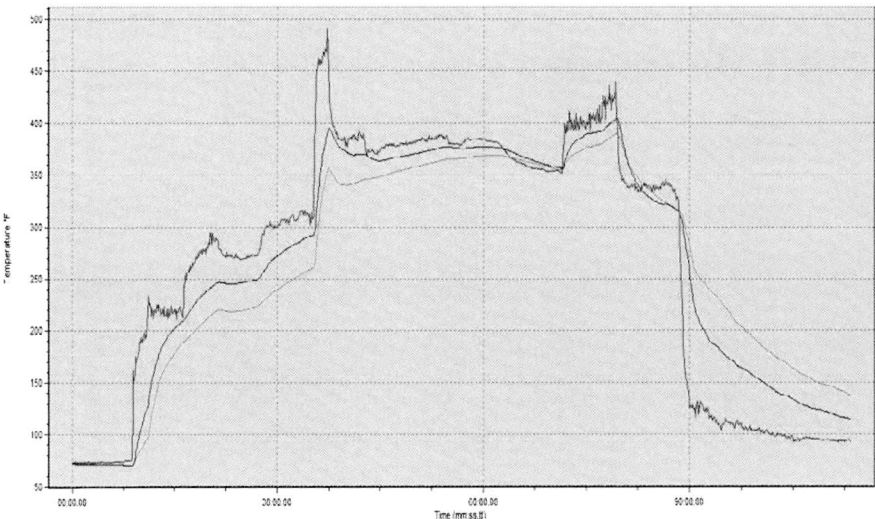

Figure 8. Furnace profile of case study before fix

The smoother profile obtained after the fix is shown in Figure 9.

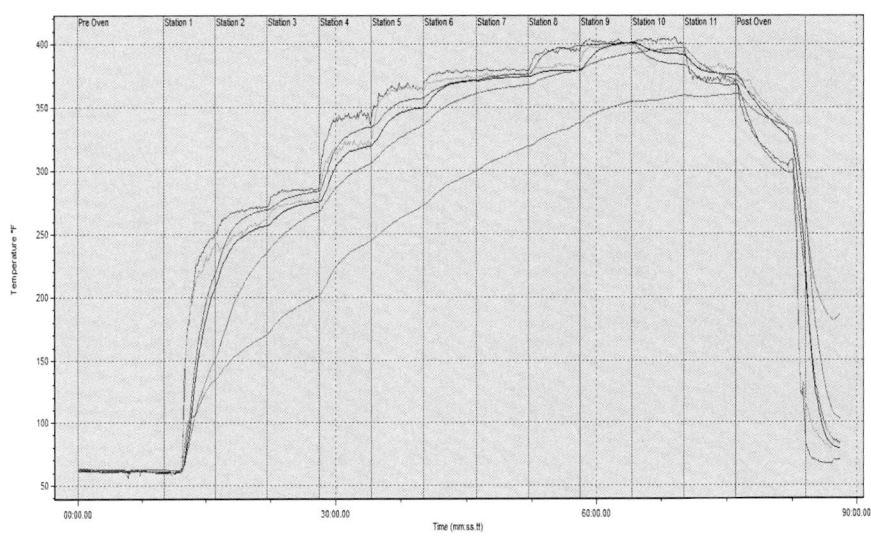

Figure 9. Furnace profile of case study after fix

In summary, run furnace profiles but also understand factors that affect temperature in the oven. These include inadequate air flow, misdirected air flow, unwanted infiltration air, poor exhaust, poorly tuned burners, and/or improperly balanced air seals.

In Process Oven Temperature Monitoring Application to Porcelain Enamel Firing

Dr Steve Offley
Datapaq Inc

Any thermal cure process can be affected by either temperature, time at temperature, or in some cases the rate of temperature change. Without any control of a curing/firing process it is possible that the product can experience either under or over temperature conditions which will deteriorate the coating quality or physical characteristics and reduce life expectancy of the coating and or product. Although ovens and furnaces have control systems they are based on control thermocouples monitoring the ambient air temperature, at limited points in the furnace, not product temperature, which is the critical parameter of interest.

Cured or Fired? If Not, Why Not?

To prove that a coated product (powder, or other) is experiencing the optimum cure schedule, it is essential that a comprehensive temperature history of the component is obtained throughout the entire thermal process. The same applies to porcelain enamels where it is essential that each product or part experiences the correct firing conditions. The only accurate safe means of obtaining such information is to employ in-process temperature profiling as shown in Figure 1. A thermally protected data logger system travels through the firing oven/furnace collecting temperature data taken from selected locations on the product. A profile graph generated by the data logger gives evidence as to the success or failure of the firing processes.

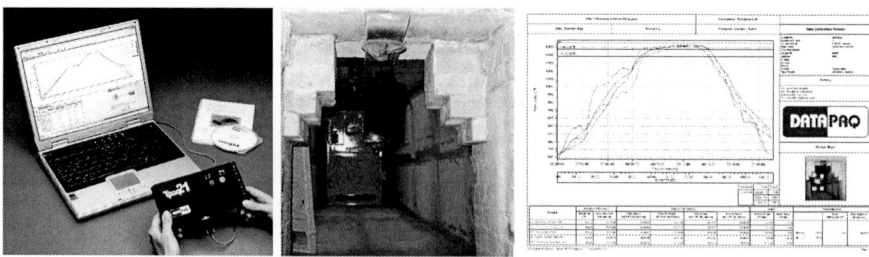

Figure 1. In-process temperature profiling

Overview

The Datapaq porcelain enamel profiling system is comprised of 4 key components (a) data logger (b) thermal barrier (c) thermocouples and (d) profile analysis software working together to provide a comprehensive thermal record of exactly what temperatures of the product as it travelled through the firing oven/furnace.

Data logger

At the heart of the profiling system the TPAQ21 data logger is designed for use in the furnace heat treatment industry for applications reaching 1000°C (1832°F) and above. It is shown in Figure 2. It is designed specifically for high temperature firing applications where the logger needs to be both tough and accurate (Logger accuracy +/- 0.3°C/0.5°F). The aluminum case protects against the rigors of furnace operation. The logger is capable of running successfully at operating temperatures up to 70°C (158°F) so even if it heats up in the thermal barrier during the run, you are confident that the data will be accurate and the logger is unharmed. Operation of the logger is simple using basic start stop buttons with comprehensive LED lights to indicate exactly what the logger is doing at any point in the process.

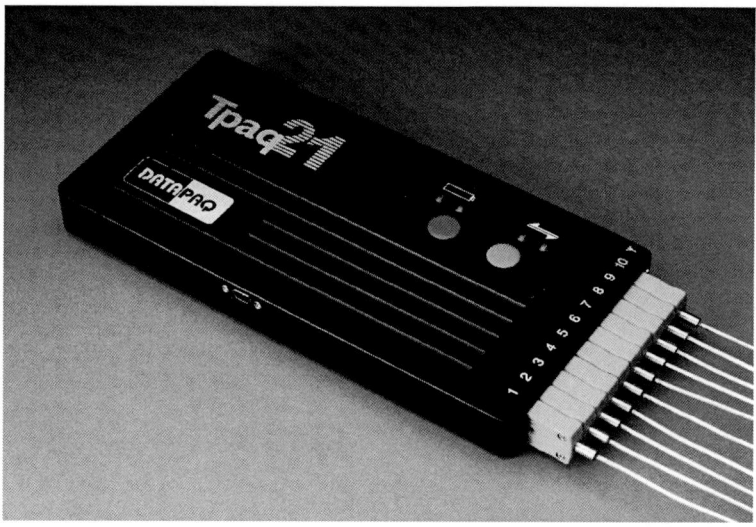

Figure 2. Datapaq TPaq21 10 Channel Data logger

The TPaq21 provides 10 thermocouple input channels allowing ten points of measurement either on the surface of the product or actually in the oven itself. With ten thermocouples it is possible to monitor the whole process in detail and ensure that all parts of the product(s) experience the same temperature. In a single profile run, confirm heating rates on parts of different thermal mass or different areas on the same part and also different locations in the oven. Remember that the heating rate of your product is not just down to your oven operation but can be affected by many other process characteristics including the following:

1. Oven starting temperature (box oven - temperature drop on loading)
2. Conveyor track speed
3. Substrate (product) thickness, weight or shape
4. Substrate material - steel or aluminum
5. Mix of components / oven loading
6. Oven design (IR, convection)
7. Furnace temperature recovery rate
8. Thermal uniformity in furnace

Thermal Barrier

As its name suggests the thermal barrier is a device used to protect the data logger as it travels through the process from the excessive temperatures of the firing oven/furnace. Obviously operating at up to 1000°C (1832°F) the performance of the thermal barrier is critical to the success of the system. To maintain the operating temperature of the data logger below 70°C (158°F) the thermal barrier employs two methods of temperature protection. The thermal barrier is shown in Figure 3. Two different sized barriers can be specified to match process conditions and space limitations: (1) TB4905 800°C (1475°F) 1.0 hour protection, (2) TB4912 800 °C (1475°F) 1.75 hours protection.

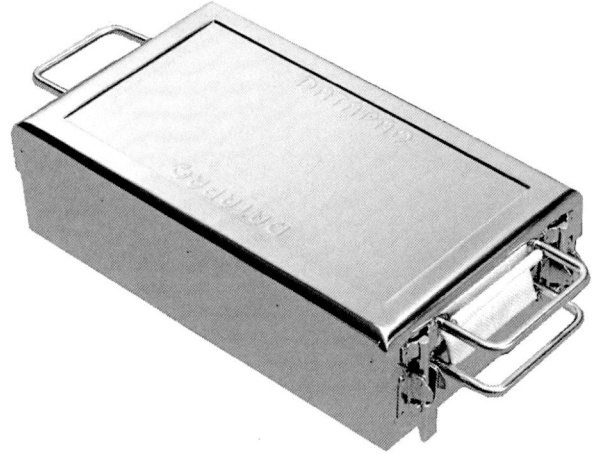

Figure 3. Datapaq TB4900 Series Thermal Barrier

The main thermal protection of the barrier is provided by micro porous insulation contained within the rugged 310 stainless steel barrier box. The insulating properties of this material slow down the heat penetration into the center of the barrier where the logger is located. A heat sink is located at the center of the barrier containing a phase change material that provides secondary thermal protection. The heat sink works by absorbing heat that reaches the logger and by going through a phase change process maintains the temperature at a safe 58°C (136°F).

The combined performance of micro porous insulation and heat sink provides typical protection at 800°C (1475°F) for between 1 and 2 hours depending on the size of the barrier. This will satisfy most porcelain enamel firing processes.

Thermocouples

A critical consideration with any temperature profile is what type of thermocouples should I use and where and how should I apply them? Faced with measuring temperatures up to 1000°C (1832°F) the choice of probe material is restricted to two basic types shown in Figure 4. The most commonly used thermocouple is the Mineral Insulated probe since it's a very robust thermocouple with a maximum operating temperature of 1250°C (2282°F). The Nicrobel sheath gives good protection against electrical "noise" and furnace atmospheres. An alternative lower temperature thermocouple choice is the Nextel Insulated thermocouple which has a Braided "Nextel" fiber insulation material. Capable of operating up to a maximum of 1000°C (1832°F), the thermocouple gives fast response but suffers from electrical noise and a possibly shorter working life.

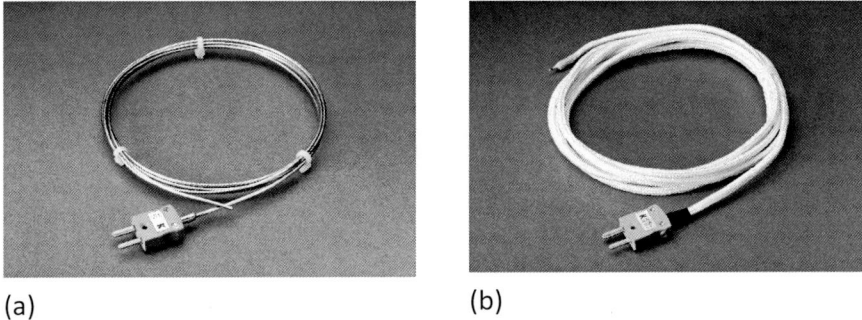

(a)   (b)

Figure 4. Datapaq thermocouples for porcelain enamel specified to ANSI MC96.1 special limits of error of +/- 0.4% or +/- 1.1°C (+/- 2.0°F): (a) Type K 1.5 mm diam mineral insulated thermocouple, probe insulation Nicrobel D, max temp 1250°C (2282°F), hot junction insulated; (b) Type K "Nextel" insulated thermocouple, probe insulation braided "Nextel" fiber, max temp 1000°C (1832°F) hot junction open

With firing operations running at up to 1000°C (1832°F), fixing thermocouples to any product is going to be a challenge. In most situations the preferred option is to take a scrap product and use it as a test piece to which the probes are permanently secured.

This method of profiling, while requiring some investment in time up front and the sacrifice of a sample product, has significant advantages. As the thermocouples are permanently fixed to the product you are guaranteed that the profile measurements are made from the same location each and every run. This removes experimental error and possible misplacement of thermocouples from run to run. If the profile changes between runs it is down to the furnace not the product or profile set-up.

Generally a physical method of securing the thermocouple is used as shown in Figure 5 to attach the thermocouple to a product and ensure good contact between the probe tip where the measurement is made and the product.

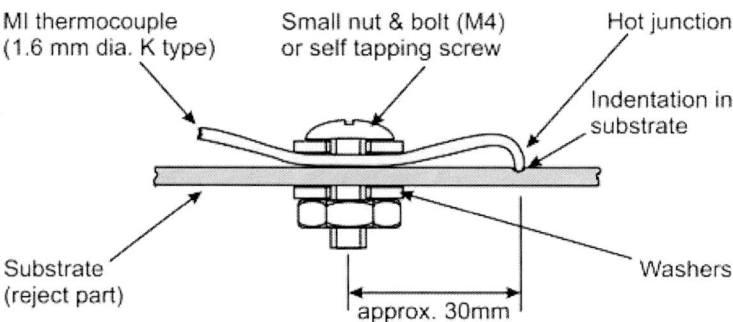

Figure 5. Datapaq thermocouples attachment to substrate using a nut or bolt to guarantee contact between the hot junction of the probe where the measurement is made and the product surface

Profile Analysis Software

Collecting the raw profile temperature data is only part of the story. After the run is completed, the data logger is connected to a laptop or PC running profile analysis software and the collected profile data is transferred for review, analysis and reporting.

Obviously the profile graph/trace (such as in Figure 6) tells the operator a lot about what is happening inside the furnace and exactly what temperatures the product has experienced. The analysis software allows raw data to be interrogated to gain an understanding of the process which will help with the control and optimization of that process.

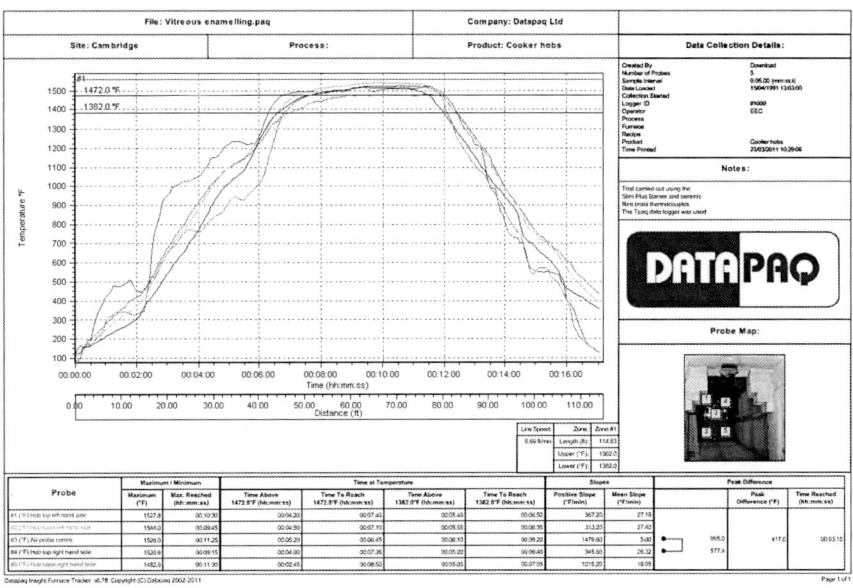

Figure 6. Datapaq Insight Software Report detailing the furnace profile and process specific analysis results used to quantify whether the firing process has been successful or not.

Typical Analysis tools applied to the profile include:

- Max temp - Quantify process hotspots or where product overheating may be a process issue

- Time at temp - Confirm that the profile satisfies the enamel firing specification

- Slopes - Control the porcelain enamel melt process and optimize throughput

- Peak difference - Identify areas of the product of significantly different thermal mass. Quantify the overall balance of temperature within the oven. Locate hot and cold spots quickly and efficiently

- Profile overlay - Immediately see the effect of changing operating parameters on the oven profile. Check how the process has changed since last run

- SPC - Analyze profile data historically to check for process control and process trending

- Area under curve - Quantify total energy used in the process

- Process files - Describe yourcomplete furnace process (zones, set-points, product photos) to add meaning to the profile graph and communicate to others what is happening.

Real Time Process Profile Capability

Conventionally the furnace profile requires that the test must be completed before the collected temperature profile data is retrieved from the data logger, post run. A recent innovation in the profile technique is the incorporation of radio telemetry into the system (Figure 7), which allows the measured data to be transferred live from the process back to the monitoring PC in real time. A radio transmitter fitted within the data logger transmits the temperature data as it is recorded via a transmitting antenna out of the furnace. The signal is detected by either a single receiver antenna (primary receiver) connected directly to the PC or a series of receivers positioned along the furnace length linked back again to the PC running the analysis software. Having access to the profile data as it happens can be very helpful with highlighting issues instantaneously, saving time and potentially preventing excessive scrap and lost production. If optimizing new processes you can see the effect of altering process characteristics immediately which may reduce the optimization set-up time significantly and reduce the number of profiles required.

Figure 7. Datapaq TM21 radio telemetry system used with the TPaq21 data logger to transmit profile data live from the firing furnace back to the analysis PC as the Datapaq system travels through the process

Temperature Profiling – The Benefits Speak for Themselves

Historically and still today, temperature profiling is employed for product coating quality assurance. With advances of information provided by profiling systems there is scope for so much more. The information provided is now helping companies improve their operating efficiency as well as understanding and control of their thermal cure/firing processes. The level of information and analysis capability now available has opened many more areas of interest and benefit such as:

- **Quality Assurance** - Confirm that all products achieve the required firing schedule to guarantee the porcelain enamel physical properties. If problems occur which may affect quality, identify them immediately.

- **Process Control** - Prove that the firing process is being performed in a controlled repeatable fashion day to day. Compare regular profile traces to see if your process is changing. Identify gradual changes over time that can be corrected without risk of line failure or expensive downtime.
- **Process Optimization** - Obtain profile information necessary for developing and validating new processes or applying new products accurately and efficiently.
- **Improved Productivity** - Eliminate rejects or rework, therefore maximizing product throughput and minimizing scrap costs.
- **Improved Efficiency** - Use profile data to understand and optimize the operating characteristics of any firing process permitting possible faster line speeds, therefore, increased product throughput or reduced operating costs.
- **Reduced Energy Consumption** - Fine tune the set-point temperatures of the furnace with confidence to reduce energy consumption without risking product quality. Create furnace programs to match product batches and different product characteristics. Determine what financial benefit reducing your furnace energy consumption by 10% could provide per annum.
- **Problem Solving** - When problems occur, identify the cause and location of the problem promptly. Use the profile information to suggest necessary corrective action and prove the success of such action with follow-on profile runs.
- **Regulatory compliance** - Archive fully traceable and certified temperature profile data and or create hard copy reports to prove to management, customers, and regulatory bodies (ISO9001) that your process complies with formal operating standards.

Conclusion

Understanding exactly what is happening in a porcelain enamel furnace is critical to the overall performance of the finished product. Knowing the exact product temperature and process temperature using the technique of in-process temperature profiling is helpful in optimizing the full potential of the firing production step. Not only can the operator guarantee product quality thus eliminating costing scrap and lost production time, but one can potentially maximize the operating characteristics of the furnace to reduce energy costs or potentially increase productivity.

Furnace Efficiency

Kevin Coursin
KMI Systems, Inc.

The factors that negatively impact furnace efficiency are reviewed.

Furnace efficiency is useful as a measurement of the furnace performance and to provide a means for determining gross input required to heat a given workload such as requirements for changing product weight or line speed changes. The definition of furnace efficiency is based upon converting chemical or electrical energy brought to it into thermal energy (heat) and then released into the furnace. This can be expressed as:

$$\text{Overall thermal efficiency} = 100 \times \frac{\text{Useful Output}}{\text{Gross Input}}$$

Where gross input is the total energy consumed by the furnace, and useful input is the total absorbed by the workload (parts & tooling).

The difference between gross input and useful output is energy consumed as heat losses such as opening losses, wall and roof losses, conveyor losses, and furnace heat storage (heating up of the furnace components to temperature at start-up).

There are several types of efficiencies. Burner efficiency is based upon the exhaust temperature from the burner tube. Furnace efficiency is based upon the exhaust temperature of the flue gas leaving the furnace. Load efficiency is based upon useful heat transferred to the ware and tools. Overall system efficiency is based upon how much heat is recovered for preheating the combustion air or how much is used in the dryer from waste heat.

Furnace heat balance is in Figure 1. This shows the different possible losses. Components of the furnace efficiency are burner efficiency, heat release of the burner tube (including surface area and uniformity of the tube), and use of waste heat from the furnace.

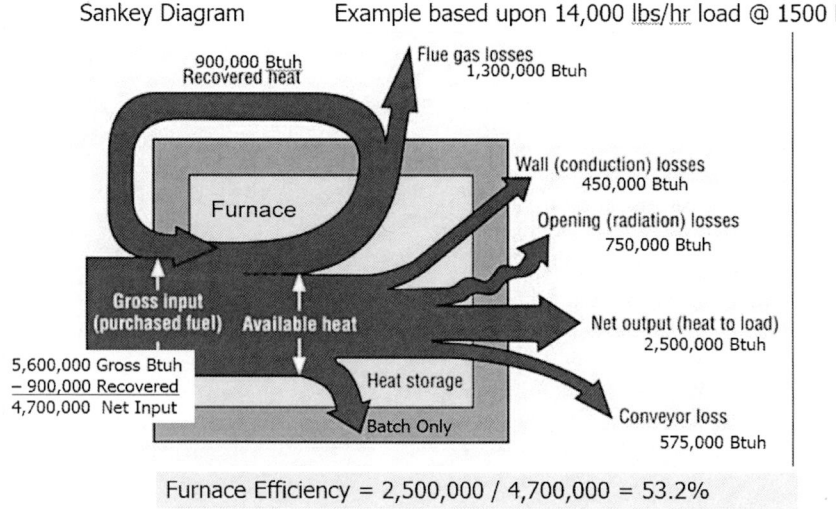

Figure 1. Furnace heat balance

Table 1 shows available heat released from the burner tubes. Heat release from the burner tubes is limited by the temperature uniformity across the entire tube so as not to have a hot spot which would exceed the temperature limit of the material. A better tube uniformity allows a higher overall tube temperature without exceeding the upper tube material limit and thus a higher heat release.

	Burner Eff.	% Available Heat	Burner Tube Heat Flux (BTU/in²)	Preheat Temp (F)	Exhaust Temp (F)
S-tube w/o preheat	55%	65%	55 tube 20 radiator	N/A	1200
S-tube w/ preheat	65%	80%	60 tube 20 radiator	850	700
Trident or U-tube w/ recuperator	55%	55%	50	600	1200
P-tube	75%	75%	55	1100	600

Table 1. Available heat released from the burner tubes

Figure 2 shows increased heat transfer through improved tube temperature uniformity.

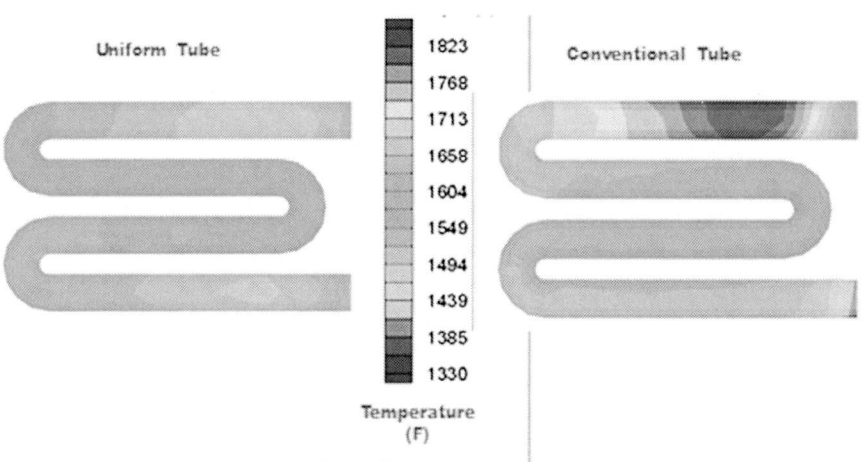

Figure 2. Tube temperature uniformity

Figure 3 shows how improved uniformity improves the maximum heat transfer capability.

Furnace Efficiency

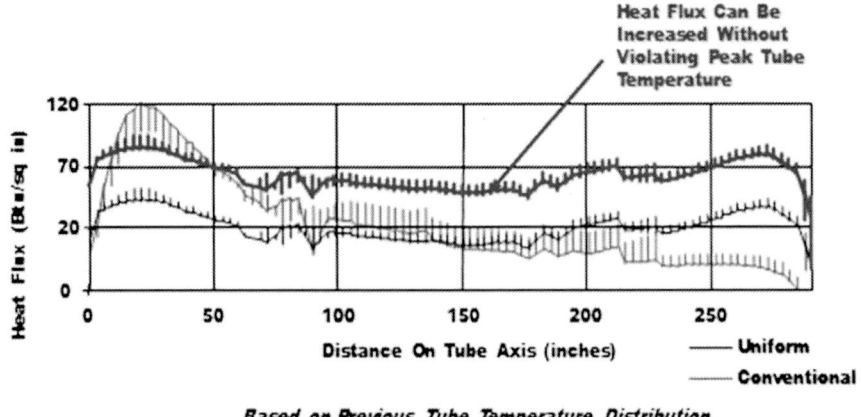

Figure 3. Uniform versus conventional heat flux comparison

The available heat output from the burner tubes is utilized in the following areas:

- ~10% Wall Losses
- ~17% Opening losses (radiation & leakage)
- ~13% Conveyor chain & trolley heat loss
- ~60% Net output to product & ware (80% product and 20% ware)

In summary, furnaces are comprised of various heating parts that all contribute to the furnace efficiency including the burners, preheated combustion or not, burner tube heat flux (heat transfer) and surface area, and waste heat use in another separate piece of equipment such as an oven or hot water generator. The ultimate energy efficiency goal of any system is to utilize all available heat. Reducing losses is very important. Several methods and types of component pieces are available, but in the end, the total system efficiency is the important part.

Recent and Developing Environmental Rules and Policies Impacting Manufacturing

Jack Waggener, P.E.
URS Corporation

EPA TSCA impact on frit

This review of recent developing environmental rules covers:

- EPA impacts of potential TSCA changes on frits
- MSDS formatting
- OSHA rules (Silica)
- Greenhouse gases (GHG)
- Other EPA air rules
- EPA solid waste and incinerator rules
- EPA wastewater and storm water rules

EPA Impacts of Potential TSCA Changes on Frits

Pre-Manufacturing Notice (PMN) could be required for all frit formulations if the frit TSCA inventory categorical mixture listing is changed. Frit is currently listed under TSCA under CAS number 65997-18-4 with the following definition:

Frit is a mixture of inorganic chemical substances produced by rapidly quenching a molten, complex combination of materials, confining the chemical substances thus manufactured as nonmigratory components of glassy solid flakes or granules. This category includes all of the chemical substances specified below when they are intentionally manufactured in the production of frit. The primary members of this category are oxides of some or all of the elements listed below. Fluorides of these elements may also be included in combination with these primary substances:

- Aluminum, Antimony, Arsenic,
- Barium, Bismuth, Boron
- Cadmium, Calcium, Cerium, Chromium, Cobalt, Copper

- Gold, Iron
- Lanthanum, Lead, Lithium
- Magnesium, Manganese, Molybdenum
- Neodymium, Nickel, Niobium
- Phosphorus, Potassium
- Silicon, Silver, Sodium, Strontium
- Tin, Titanium, Tungsten
- Vanadium
- Zinc, Zirconium

This categorical inventory listing has been in effect legally for more than 30 years. No risks have been articulated. Unintended consequences of removing the frit category inventory listing would be:

- Undue PMN burden on industry
- Uncertain analytical instrument requirements and nomenclature rules
- Lengthened agency review periods due to additional PMN load
- Adverse impact on innovative and replacement products for a number of large markets critical to the U.S. economy
- Adverse impacts to DoD and DoE

In 2011 and 2012 there were many meetings and correspondence with EPA and OMB through the American Chemistry Council Industry Coalition. Any early prediction was this would gain traction in early 2013 after the election, but, as of May 2013, the EPA seems to have stalled.

MSDS Formatting

MSDS Formatting will be globally harmonized under United Nations rule. By June 1, 2015, all Safety Data Sheets (SDS) need to comply with amended provisions. December 1, 2013 is the deadline to train employees on new labels, elements and the SDS format.

OSHA Rules (Silica)

This is a new OSHA initiative with potential for impact to PEI. There was a notice of proposed rulemaking in the summer of 2013 to change the permissible exposure limit (PEL) of crystalline silica from 100 µg/m^3. The options are 25, 50, 75, or 100 µg/m^3. Impacts would be changes to equipment line, protective work clothing, respiratory protection, hygiene facilities and practices, and employee health screening. There are potential compliance issues for companies. There is substantial non-compliance with the current standard in some industries, and a lower standard would be hard for many to meet. Poor analytical capability makes it hard to measure exposures lower than current PEL; the action level would be even more difficult.

Greenhouse Gases (GHG)

The Mandatory GHG Reporting Rule on September 22, 2009 impacted industries emitting 25,000 MT or more per year of GHGs including those from gas ovens/furnaces (but not electrics yet), fuel suppliers (natural gas, refineries, etc.), automotive and steel. Monitoring and reporting began January 1, 2010 with the first report for year 2010 due September 31, 2011.

The final "tailoring" rule is in progress for GHG permitting existing toxics threshold of 100 and 250 Tons/yr (not reasonable for GHG). EPA has proposed 25,000 tons of CO_2. The final rule (June 3, 2010) had 75,000 tons per year increase. New permits are being challenged. The US Congress is pushing back, and there have been court appeals.

Other EPA Air Rules

Boiler MACT (finalized on January 31, 2013)
- Major sources
- 14,000 major source boilers

- Excludes process heaters
- Existing sources must comply by January 31, 2016
- Initial notification due by May 31, 2013

Boiler area source rule
- Smaller units
- 183,000 area source boilers
- Initial notification extended until January 20, 2014
- Initial tune-up extended until March 21, 2014 (existing units)
- Tune-ups every 5 years instead of every 2 years

Commercial industrial solid waste incinerator (CISWI)
- Revised rule after election...3 to 5 yrs. To comply 106 units

Non-hazardous solid materials (NHSM)
- Revised rule 2013...definitions
- Used Oil

Other air rules for utilities will impact manufacturing:

- ❖ Steam electric power MACT rule (final)
  - ➢ Targets coal and fuel oil
  - ➢ Move to natural gas and other
  - ➢ Regulates Hg, Se, SO_2, etc.
  - ➢ Co-rule: wastewater rules
- ❖ Proposed utility GHG rule for new sources
  - ➢ Targets coal and fuel oil
  - ➢ Move to natural gas
- ❖ This means cost increases to the enameller
  - ➢ 50%+ power plants use coal

EPA Solid Waste and Incinerator Rules

There is the impact of the final EPA solid waste and incinerator rule. In the past, press pit/forming oils may have been recovered and used for energy recovery at a small cost to the enameling plant. In the future, these will be a solid waste (due to chlorinated parrafins) to be burned in an incinerator at ten times the past cost, which is problematic to stainless steel.

EPA Wastewater and Storm water Rules

New wastewater and storm water EPA rules for low impact development (LID) and green infrastructure will impact your facility. The post-construction storm water rule was published in the Federal Register notice on Dec. 28, 2009. The distributed information collection request was in 2010. A small business panel was held in the Fall of 2010 involving EPA, OMB, SBA, and SER's, SBREFA: Small Business Regulatory Enforcement Act of 1996. The timeline of the post-construction storm water rule that promotes LID and green building:

- Published Federal Register notice (Dec. 28, 2009)
- Propose revised rule by Summer 2013 (?)
- Final action by December 10, 2014 (?)

Increasing urbanization increases stormwater runoff by decreasing the infiltration through natural ground cover. Various green infrastructure approaches include:

- Green roof
- Rain garden
- Parking lot infiltration island
- Open swale
- Terraced open swale
- Porous pavement sidewalk
- Porous pavers
- Large cisterns

Standards are also being established for discharges from newly developed and re-developed sites using LID and development. The goal is to maintain or restore hydrology, water quality in receiving waters, and recharge groundwater to maintain predevelopment runoff levels. The standard could include:

- On-site retention of a specific size storm event (e.g., 2-year, 24-hour storm (i.e., 3.0 to 3.5 inches in East))
- Retain 95% Rain Event (i.e., approx. 1.5 inches in East)

The bottom line estimated cost impact of the storm water rules is shown below:

Rule	Estimate
Post Construction Rule Based on 2 yr. – 24 hrs. Storm Being Retained by LID	$100K/acre ± + Cost of Land
C&D ELG (280 NTU)	$40K/acre
Total	$140K/acre + Cost of Land

Finally, there has been good news regarding wastewater effluent limitation guidelines (ELG). The EPA Evaluates ELGs every two years to determine if revisions are needed:

- Porcelain Enamel: "No Action" (original in 1970's and 80's)
- Metal Finishing: "No Action" (original in 1980's)
- Metal Products & Machinery: "No Action" (original in 2003)

General Concepts for the Production of Enameling Steel

Robert Yap
Nucor Steel-Berkeley

Steel making at Nucor Steel-Berkeley is reviewed with basic steel concepts. Common enameling defects are described with their most common solutions.

Steel Making

Figure 1 shows the Nucor Steel mill in Berkeley. The raw materials used are heavy metal scrap, scrap bundles, shredded scrap, hot briquetted iron (HBI), or pig iron. The melt shop contains an electric arc furnace (EAF), ladle metallurgy furnace (LMF), a degasser (required for certain grades), and a continuous caster. Hot rolled (HR) steel is made at the hot mill. The cold mill does cold rolling, annealing, and temper passing. The galvanized product is not used for enameling.

Figure 1. Nucor Steel-Berkeley

The purpose of the electric arc furnace (EAF) shown in Figure 2 is to melt solid scrap and iron into liquid steel. It is a DC furnace charged with 180 tons of scrap, iron, and flux. It takes approximately 30-40 minutes to melt 1 heat of steel. The bottom tap sends 160-170 tons of liquid steel into a ladle. The typical operation temperature is 2950°F with a total melt capacity of over 3 million tons/year.

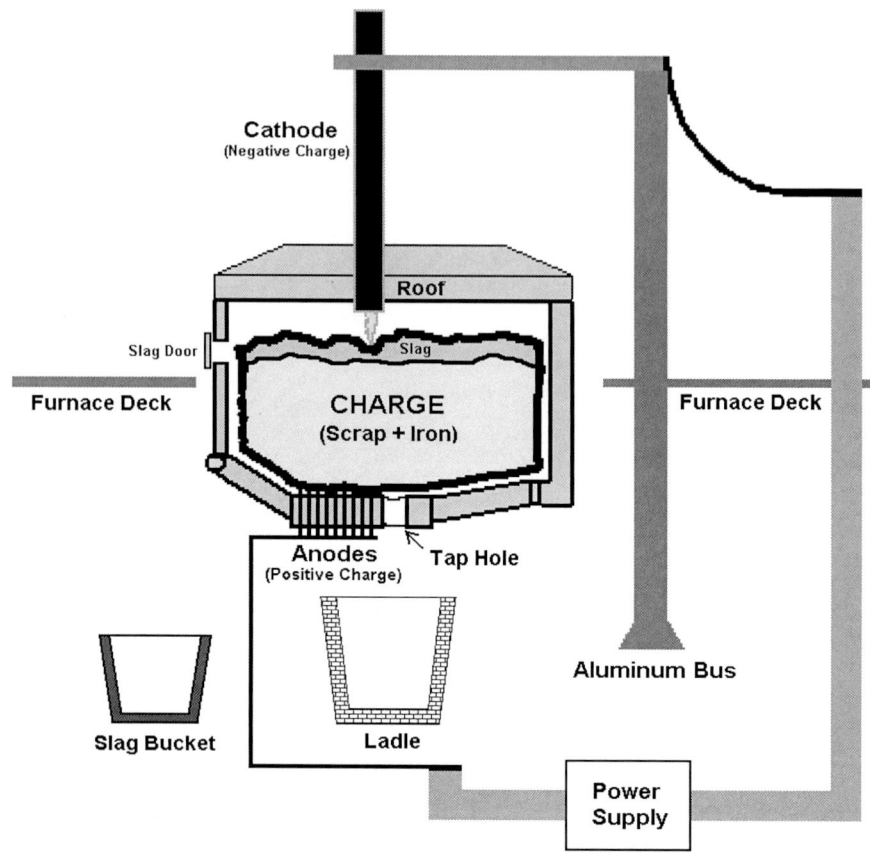

Figure 2. Electric arc furnace (EAF)

The Ladle Metallurgy Furnace (LMF) in Figure 3 modifies the chemistry to make a specific steel grade. It is an AC furnace with argon stirring. Inclusions can be modified. The typical temperature is 2900°F.

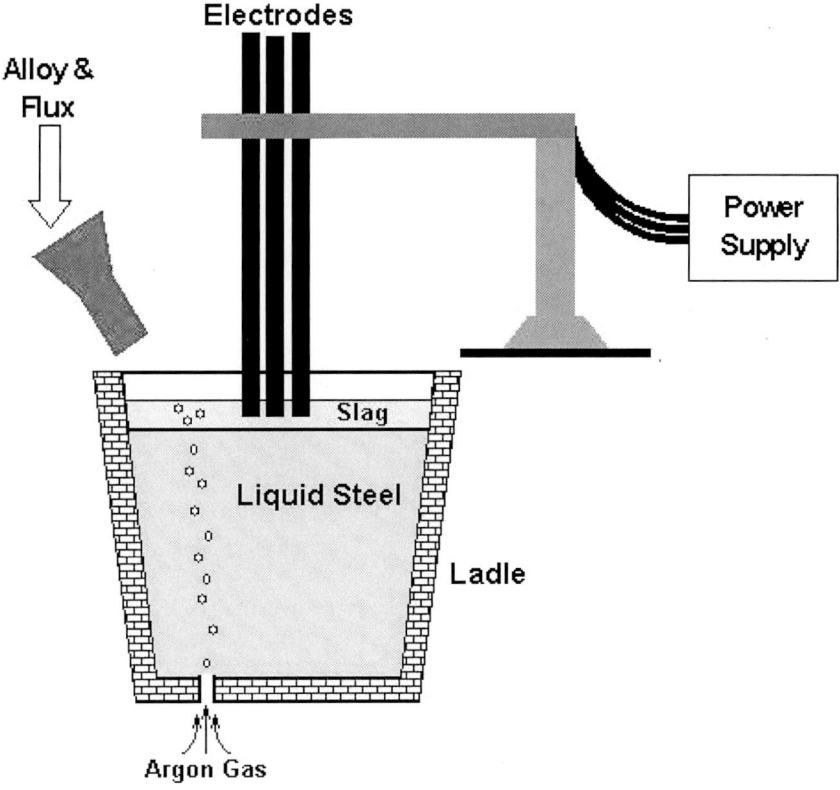

Figure 3. Ladle metallurgy furnace (LMF)

Shown in Figure 4, the vacuum tank degasser reduces carbon, hydrogen, and nitrogen required for some grades. It operates with a pressure drop from 15 psi to 0.015 psi. Nucor Steel-Berkeley was the first mini-mill to have a production degasser.

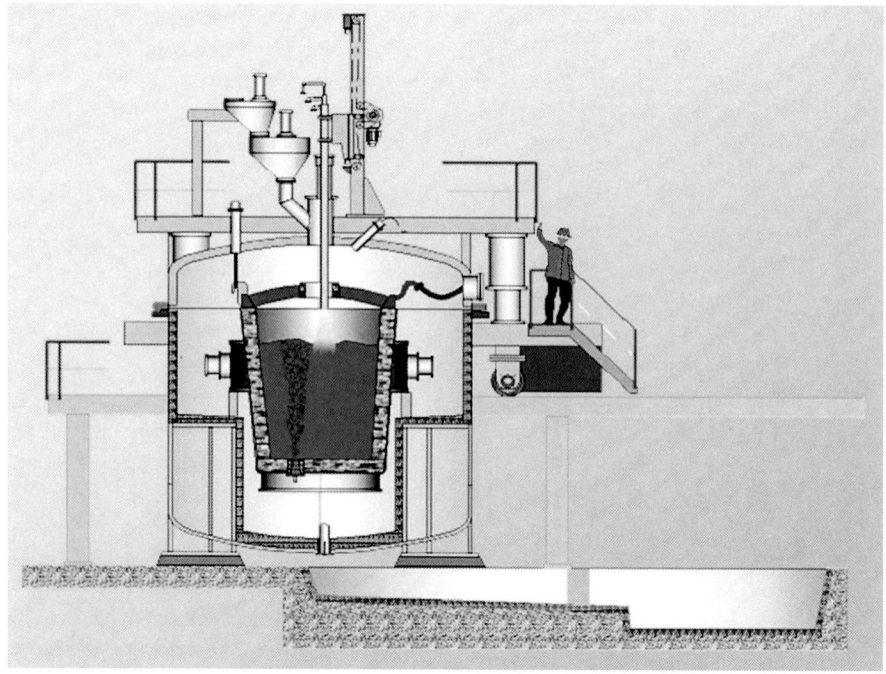

Figure 4. Vacuum tank degasser

Continuous casting (Figure 5) converts liquid steel into solid steel (i.e., makes slabs). A thin, solid steel shell is formed in the mold containing the liquid core. As the steel passes through the segments it completely solidifies. The typical casting rate for Nucor Steel with 2" thick slab is 200 in/min, and the typical slab exit temperature is 1800 to 1900°F.

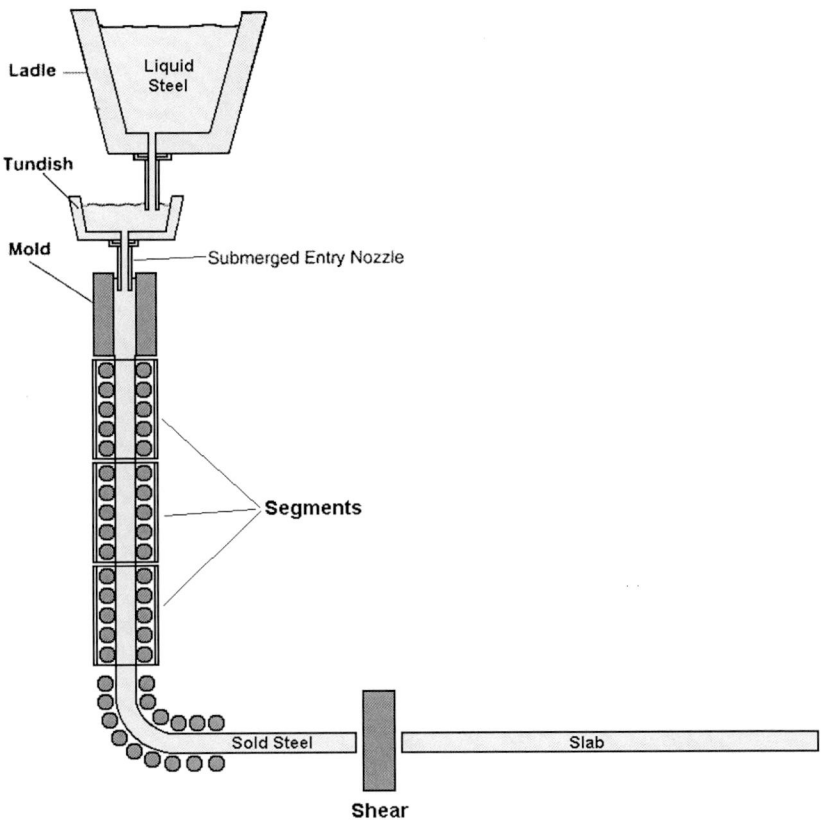

Figure 5. Continuous casting

The purpose of the hot mill in Figure 6 is to roll a slab into a hot roll coil. The slab emerges from tunnel furnace at 2100°F then passes through a descaler (4,000 psi water spray, top and bottom). Next, it moves through a 4-high, 6-stand finishing mill to reach a thickness range of 0.057 to 0.625 in. The temperature changes at each stand can change mechanical properties. The typical finishing temperature is 1,650°F, and the typical coiling temperature is 1,200°F. The hot mill has a capacity of producing over 50,000 tons/week of HR coils.

General Concepts for the Production of Enameling Steel

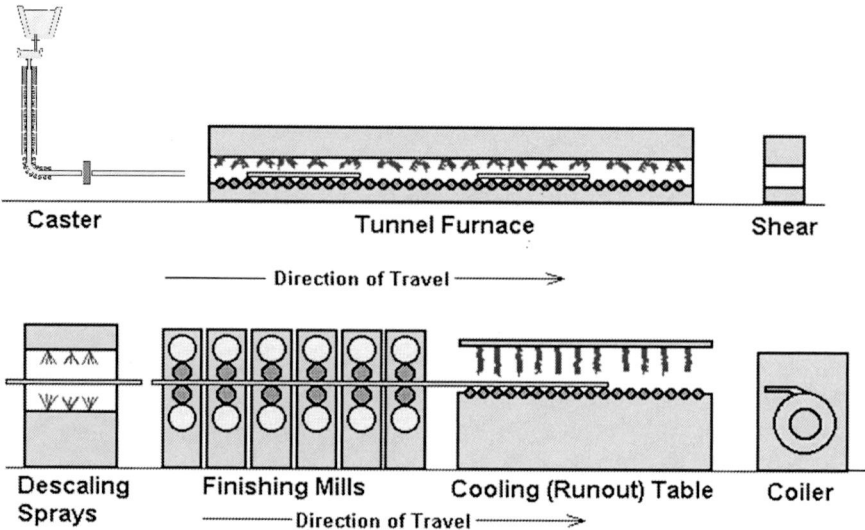

Figure 6. Hot mill

In Figure 7, pickling makes a HRPO coil by removing the iron oxide (scale) with hydrochloric acid (HCl). A push/pull pickle line is used. Edge trimming is done to width (cut edge).

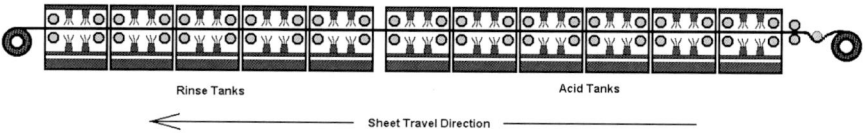

Figure 7. Pickling

Cold rolling (reversing mill) in Figure 8 rolls a HRPO coil to create a CRFH coil using a 4-high, single-stand, reversing mill. There are typically 3 to 5 passes through the mill that reduce thickness by up to 85%. Reduction is achieved through roll force (up to 1,800 tons) and tension. A uniform thickness throughout the coil is the result, and the steel is extremely strong after cold-rolling but has very little ductility.

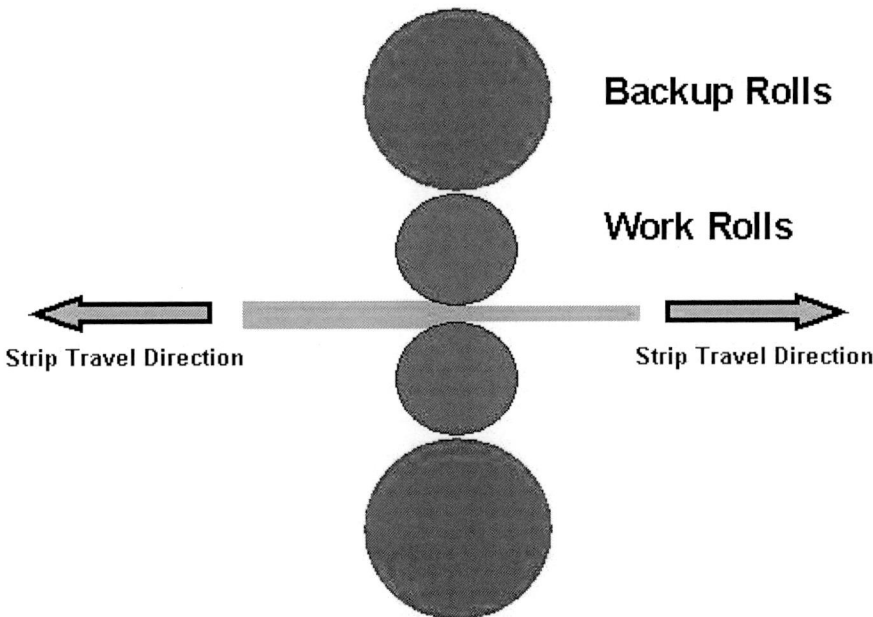

Figure 8. Cold rolling (reversing mill)

The purpose of batch process annealing in Figure 9 is to soften a CRFH coil. Primary heat transfer is by convection using a hydrogen atmosphere. Natural gas combustion is done outside of the inner cover using direct flame or radiant tubes. The typical gas temperature is 1,400°F with a cycle time of 2-3 days. The steel is very soft after annealing. The microstructure undergoes recovery, recrystallization and grain growth to achieve desired mechanical properties.

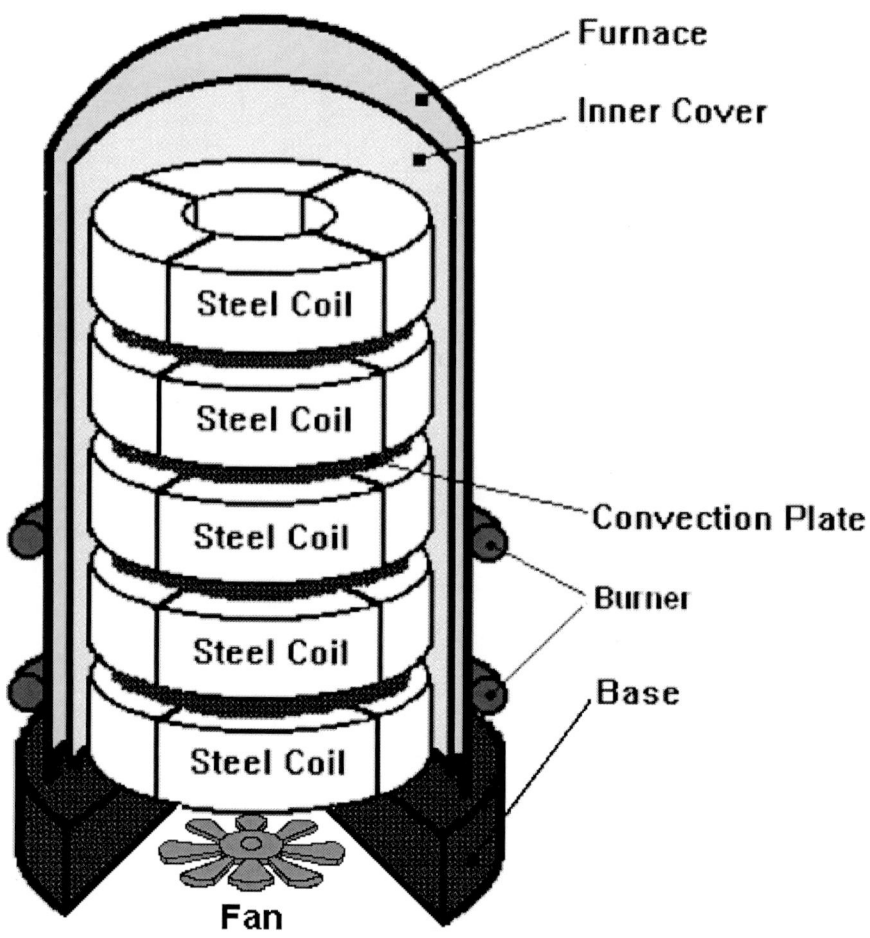

Figure 9. Annealing process

Shown in Figure 10, temper passing slightly increases the mechanical properties of an annealed coil to prevent defects caused by the steel being too soft. A single pass through a 4-high, single-stand mill is done. Extensions are typically 1%-2%. This imparts the desired surface roughness (matte or textured), and improves the shape.

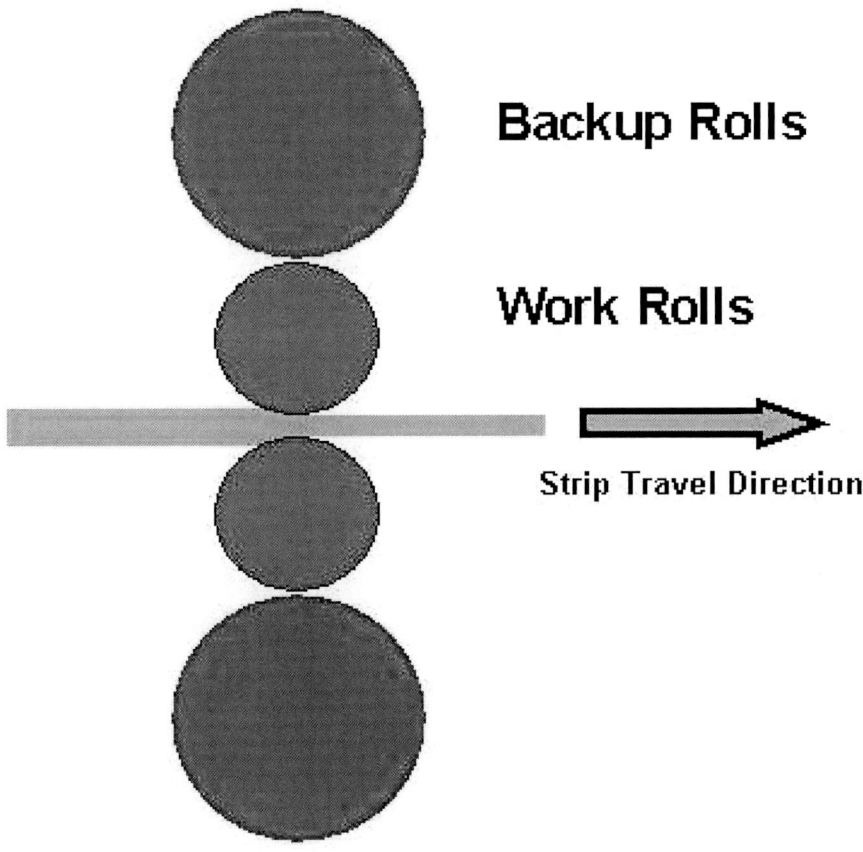

Figure 10. Temper passing

Enameling Defects

ASTM standard A-424 provides the acceptable range of chemistries for Type 1, 2, and 3 enameling-grade steels. Steel showing problems can be analyzed and compared to these chemistries. Besides the chemistry, the iron allotrope and steel microstructure are important. As shown in Figure 11, the iron allotrope present depends on temperature and the percentage of carbon. A binary phase diagram like the one shown is a map of the equilibrium states of an alloy over different compositions and temperatures. Nearly pure steel is ferrite a-iron. Austenite (g-iron) is a solid solution that form with increased carbon levels. At a lower temperature range, carbon precipitates out as carbide in an a-iron matrix.

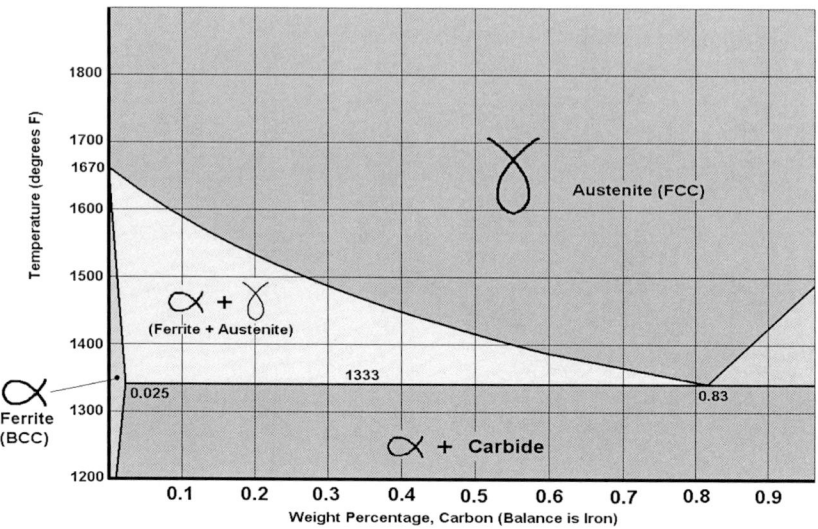

Figure 11. Iron-carbon phase diagram

Steel related enamel defects include fish scale, carbon boiling, sag/warpage, and low Strength-After-Fire (SAF). When such defects occur, the steel chemistry, iron-carbon phase diagram, hydrogen solubility in iron, and steel microstructure should be considered. Particular consideration has to be given to the potential negative effects of hydrogen or carbides on the steel. The different levels of hydrogen solubility in the iron allotropes are in Figure 12. The solubility of hydrogen is significantly lower in the lower temperature phases.

General Concepts for the Production of Enameling Steel

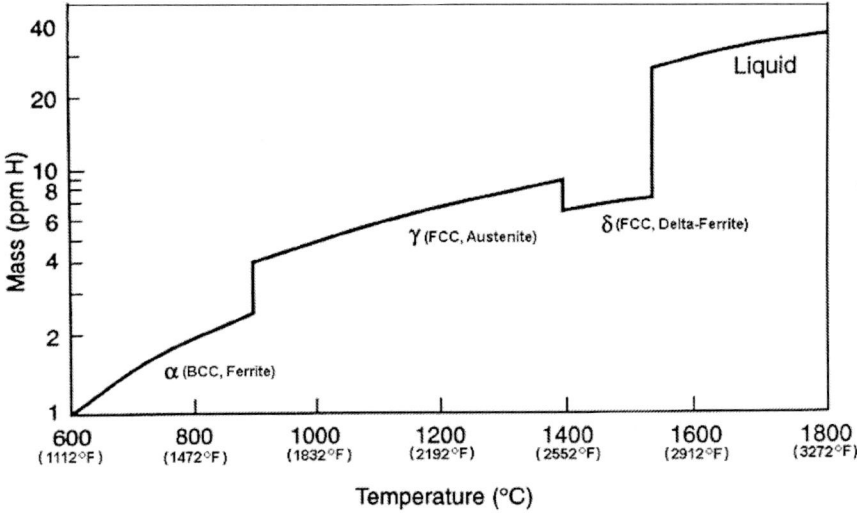

Figure 12. Solubility of hydrogen in iron at 1 atm pressure of H_2

The root cause of fish scale is hydrogen evolution from steel after firing that breaks the glass coating. The solution is to create micro-voids within the steel to act as hydrogen traps. This is done in different manners depending on which ASTM A-424 grade steel is being used. For Type I, micro-voids are formed during open coil annealing. With Type II, micro-voids are formed from carbides. With Type III, micro-voids are formed from titanium-nitrides. An SEM micrograph of a Type III Ti-N precipitate is in Figure 13.

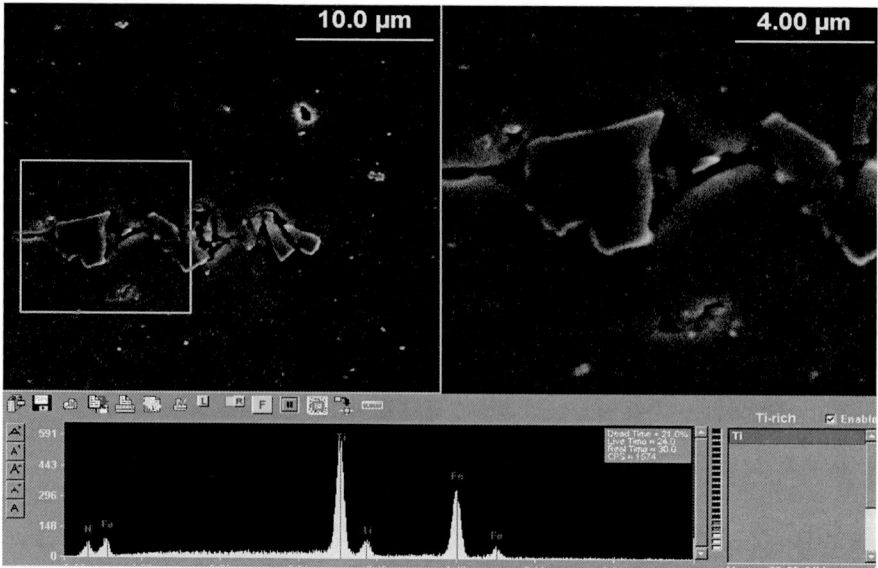

Figure 13. Type III Ti-N precipitate

Carbon boiling is caused by carbides at the surface converting to carbon monoxide (CO) gas during firing. This is solved by eliminating or minimizing carbides at the surface of steel. Sag/warpage is caused by volume changes from thermal expansion and phase changes during firing and cooling. It is addressed by limiting the carbon content to avoid phase changes. Poor Strength-After-Fire (SAF) occurs because of microstructural changes during firing and cooling. Chemistry modifications are made to retain strength after firing. The effects of different alloying elements are in Figure 14.

CARBON (C)
Increases hardness
Increasing depth of hardening
Increases tensile strength
Increases abrasion resistance
Reduces ductility and toughness

PHOSPHORUS (P)
Increases depth of hardening
Increases corrosion resistance
Improves machinability
Increases hardness, YS and TS
Increases brittleness

SILICON (Si)
Deoxidizes steel
Increases hardness
Increases YS & TS
Improves hardenability
Decreases machinability

CHROMIUM (Cr)
Increases hardness
Increases toughness
Increases depth of hardening
Increases resistance to corrosion
Increases resistance to abrasion
Increases tensile strength

VANADIUM (V)
Increases hardness
Increases yield strength
Increases depth of hardening
Inhibits age hardening
Increase tensile strength

COPPER (Cu)
Increases resistance to corrosion
Increases electrical resistance
Increases hardenabilty
Causes hot shortness during casting

MANGANESE (Mn)
Increases hardness
Increases toughness
Deoxidizes
Increases depth of hardening
Increases tensile strength

SULPHUR (S)
Improves machinability
Decreases ductility
Decreases toughness
Decreases weldability
Increases brittleness

ALUMINUM (Al)
Deoxidizes steel
Increases hardness slightly
Increases strength slightly
Retards grain growth
Retards age hardening

NICKEL (Ni)
Increases toughness
Increases tensile strength
Increases hardnes
Increases corrosion resistance

TITANIUM (Ti)
Deoxidizes steel
Retards grain growth
Retards age hardening
Increases hardenability
Increases tensile strength

BORON (B)
Increases depth of hardness
Increases hardenability
Decreases strength slightly

Figure 14. Chemistry effects on steel

Summary

The steel making processes at Nucor Steel's Berkeley mill were reviewed. The effect of the steel chemistry, particularly hydrogen and carbon, on steel-related enamel defects was discussed.

Author Index

Allison, P., 75

Baldwin, C., 1, 89

Carlson, J., 33
Coursin, K., 165

Delbaere, P., 21
De Soete, J., 21
Doak, M., 89
Dooley, R., 135

Holton, S., 75
Horton, M., 39
Hughes, L., 27

Iwamura, H., 51

Kaluzny, K., 111
Kuwae, S., 51

Malone, P., 75
McKinley, K., 1
Melaro, J., 27
Moser, R., 75

O'Connor, J., 115
Offley, S., 153
Onishi, H., 51

Palattella, P., 89
Patel, S., 123
Potter, B., 1

Rozdilsky, B., 145

Skovron, W., 45
Studnicka, J., 119

Tracey, M., 51

Voss, E., 55

Waggener, J., 169
Weiss, C., 75
Williams, B., 75

Yap, R., 175